822.6
SHE

SHERIDAN

Rivals

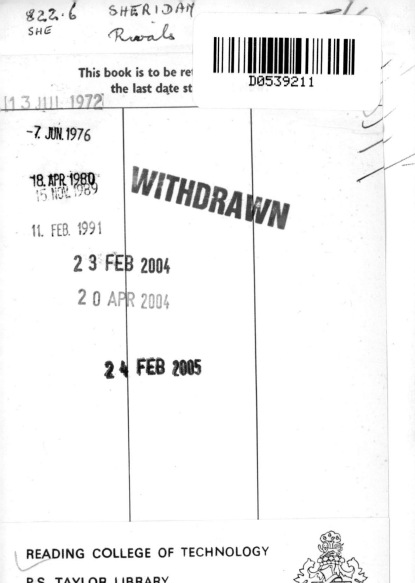

This book is to be ret...
the last date st...

D0539211

[1 3 JUL 1972]

-7. JUN. 1976

18. APR. 1980
15. NOV. 1989

11. FEB. 1991

WITHDRAWN

2 3 FEB 2004

2 0 APR 2004

2 4 FEB 2005

READING COLLEGE OF TECHNOLOGY

P.S. TAYLOR LIBRARY

KING'S ROAD

READING RG1 4HJ

ANCORA IMPARO

SHERIDAN

THE RIVALS

SHERIDAN

THE RIVALS

EDITED WITH INTRODUCTION AND

NOTES BY

T. BALSTON

OXFORD

AT THE CLARENDON PRESS

Oxford University Press, Amen House, London E.C.4

GLASGOW   NEW YORK   TORONTO   MELBOURNE   WELLINGTON
BOMBAY   CALCUTTA   MADRAS   KARACHI   KUALA LUMPUR
CAPE TOWN   IBADAN   NAIROBI   ACCRA

READING
TECHNICAL
COLLEGE
LIBRARY

6104

FIRST PUBLISHED 1913
REPRINTED 1916, 1917, 1918, 1920, 1925, 1930
1933, 1942, 1944, 1946, 1948, 1951, 1955, 1960

PRINTED IN GREAT BRITAIN

822.6
SHE

CONTENTS

INTRODUCTION

OF the only three plays in the English language, besides those of Shakespeare, which have achieved permanent popularity, two, *The School for Scandal* and *The Rivals*, are by Sheridan : the third, *She Stoops to Conquer*, is by Oliver Goldsmith. However long the interval, the name of Sheridan comes second to Shakespeare's on the roll of English dramatists.

Richard Brinsley Sheridan was born in 1751 at Dublin, where his father, an actor, was manager of the Theatre Royal. His mother was a successful novelist and playwright. The family moved to England some years later, and Richard was educated for six years at Harrow School (1762–8). His mother died in 1766. In 1770 he went to Bath, where his father hoped to live by giving lessons in elocution, and there he met Elizabeth Linley, then in her sixteenth year, but already becoming famous for her beauty and her singing. Two years later, when she decided to fly abroad from the persecutions of her admirers, especially of one married scoundrel, Major Mathews, Sheridan was chosen as her escort. On their arrival in Dunkirk he refused to leave her in a convent, as she had intended, unless previously she married him. She seems to have consented readily enough, and the marriage was performed by a Catholic priest. Soon afterwards Mr. Linley arrived in pursuit and took his daughter back to Bath. A few months later, after two duels with Mathews, Sheridan reconciled her father, married her a second time, and took her to live with him in London. The same year, 1773, *She Stoops to Conquer* was produced. Ever since he left school Sheridan had been busy with his pen, and in November 1774 he was able to announce to his father-in-law that a comedy by him would shortly be rehearsed at Covent Garden. This comedy, *The Rivals*, was actually produced on January 17 following, and for various reasons, sufficiently stated in Sheridan's preface, proved a failure. A revised version, presented eleven days later, achieved an immediate and permanent success.

At the time when Sheridan began to write there were only two living forms of drama, the Comedy of Manners and the Sentimental Comedy. Of these the Comedy of Manners, so called from the limitation of its subject-matter to the superficial habits and behaviour of society, had arisen with Ben Jonson, and passed through a heyday of extraordinary brilliance and licentiousness with the dramatists of the Restoration. But after the departure of the Stuarts the standard of public decency rose higher, and Jeremy Collier's timely pamphlet, *A Short View of the Immorality and Profaneness of the English Stage* (1698), chastised the dramatists into less reckless moods. Richard Steele, the essayist, was the first to import the new spirit into his drama, and made sentiment and morality take the place of profligacy. The sentiment, however, soon degenerated into sentimentality and the morality into Utopian nonsense, and the stage was held by the 'goddess of the woful countenance—the sentimental Muse', until in 1773 the reaction at last began. Foote's production of a burlesque sentimental comedy at the Haymarket, and Goldsmith's

of *She Stoops to Conquer* at Covent Garden, re-estab-
lished the Comedy of Manners, shorn, however, of its
previous indecency.

That Sheridan would throw in his lot with the re-
actionaries must seem inevitable to any readers of his
life : he was too virile, too sensible, too gay to find
satisfaction in the ' floods of tears '. His *Rivals* is,
of course, a Comedy of Manners, and not only that, but,
apart from certain scenes which will be considered later,
Comedy of Manners in its extremest form, pushed, as
it were, to its logical conclusion. It is, for instance, of
the essence of this Comedy to be unphilosophical, that
is, to propound no views of human life or destiny : in
The Rivals there is not the slightest suggestion of the
author's views. It is of its essence, again, to touch but
lightly on the surface of human character, to leave its
depth unsounded, its complications unresolved, to play
with its ' persons ' as with puppets : no one pulls the
wires so dexterously as Sheridan. Hardly making a
pretence of portraying human beings, he takes some single
characteristic and shows it as it would act, so to speak,
in vacuo, unconditioned by any of the other qualities
which always modify its operation in real life. His
characters are personified ' humours ' and no more,
and lest any one should fail to perceive it, he labels
them Absolute, Languish, O'Trigger, and so on. They
are like masks, each with one fixed distortion of the
human features : no individual person seems to be
behind them : their utterances are words and little more.
But these are merely the limitations, the negative
definitions of this Comedy. Its essence, on the positive
side, is to be witty and ingenious and plausible, and
here again Sheridan is superlative, most witty, most

ingenious, most plausible. His characters (and this has been a stumbling-block to many) seem to be incapable of commonplace : high and low revel in every form of wit. And his plot is not only so ingenious that each character seems to be found in every possible variety of situation, but also so plausibly constructed, that if a moment's credence be given to their existence the story seems almost to tell itself, so probable, so inevitable is the progress of events.

In short, *The Rivals* is a masterpiece of dramatic art, which can hardly have been surpassed by any other dramatist. It is not meant to assert that its value is comparable to that of any of the greatest works of human genius. We do not esteem cathedrals the less because we find more perfection in some little shrine. Few, probably, can read a play of Shakespeare's without many alterations suggesting themselves to their minds, rightly or wrongly, as improvements : few would wish to alter many words of Sheridan.

> That low man seeks a little thing to do,
>   Sees it and does it :

and within his limits Sheridan has done what he intended. To condemn him, as has been often done, because he is trivial and superficial, because he arouses no deep emotion or thought, is to condemn all irresponsible amusement. For, if the dramatist may step down from the prophet's pedestal, as even the greatest dramatists have done, how far may he descend ? May he be as irresponsible as Shakespeare, but not more so ? Or may he aim simply at amusing us ? Certainly he will find most of us grateful, if he succeeds.

Another charge which has been brought against

Sheridan is that of plagiarism, and the accusation has
been supported by a hundred pieces of evidence. The
defence, however, is now as familiar as it is conclusive.
A work of art is not, any more than a human being or
a vegetable, a spontaneous growth, unconditioned by
the time and place and circumstances of its creation.
It is born with a literary ancestry, and it can escape
no more easily or completely from its ancestral traditions
than a man from the traditions of his family. It no
more detracts from Sheridan's genius to point out resem-
blances to Wycherley or Congreve than it would smirch
the reputation of a peer to bear a likeness to the founder
of his family. And even if the resemblance is something
more than the outcome of tradition, the comparative
study of literature has shown that direct borrowing,
so far from being unpermissible, has given us some of
its finest passages. It required but a few touches to
transform an extract from a prose translation of Plutarch
into the magnificent description of the barge of Cleopatra
—as Shakespearean a passage as any in the plays. With
regard to Sheridan as to Shakespeare, the only legitimate
question is whether he assimilated what he borrowed ;
and in both cases the answer is unhesitating. The plays
of Sheridan are throughout essentially and characteris-
tically the work of Sheridan. Even Mrs. Malaprop,
whom he lifted almost bodily from his mother's unpub-
lished play, *A Journey to Bath*, has become part and parcel
of his work. His real originality lies in the completeness
and individuality of his work without any reference to its
sources or its predecessors ; and individuality in works
of art, as in human beings, is seen in the strength and
clearness of the impressions they make on others. If
an artist has welded his material into a complete organic

whole in which nothing is superfluous or lacking, he has achieved a work of art.

There are parts, however, of *The Rivals* which are now generally considered to be blemishes and to sink below the more uniform excellence of *The School for Scandal* : these are the scenes between Julia and Faulkland. I have no doubt that the sentimentality of these characters, especially of Faulkland, has been greatly exaggerated, by contemporaries for praise, and by posterity for blame. Faulkland, indeed, is a true sentimentalist of the school generally condemned by Sheridan, but in all the scenes in which he appears without Julia, and, I believe, in those too in which he appears with her, he is treated in a spirit of genuine comedy : his 'humour' rouses much less sympathy than laughter. Julia, however, is never laughable, except in so far as she heightens the ludicrousness of Faulkland, and it seems probable that she was devised as a sop to the Drury Lane audience's passion for sentimentality. Sheridan felt he could not afford to neglect this road to favour, and yet could not forbear to laugh at his sentimentalists. The result of the divided aim has been indifferent success. It jars us now to suspect sometimes that Julia and Faulkland are being treated seriously, as it jarred contemporaries to suspect them laughed at.

One further point should be considered. To pretend, as has frequently been done, that either the plot or the characters or the dialogue of *The Rivals* bear any exact resemblance to Sheridan's own 'rivalry' of 1773 is to misunderstand Sheridan and art alike. Of course, Sheridan's own intrigue threw light upon intrigue for him, his own duels illuminated duelling, his own tyrannical father illustrated the 'absolute' temperament. But that is merely to say that he was writing about the sort of life and persons with which he was acquainted, as every artist must, not that he was writing auto-biography. 'The less Shakespeare he' is the finest criticism of a long and endless controversy, not only about Shakespeare, but about all other authors. And in this special case as far as the facts are known, there is peculiarly little resemblance between the circumstances of Sheridan's marriage and those of his drama.

A few words may be said of Sheridan's later history. In 1775, four months after *The Rivals*, his *St. Patrick's Day* was produced at Covent Garden, and later *The Duenna*. In 1776 he bought Garrick's share in Drury Lane, and became its manager. In 1777 he produced his *Trip to Scarborough* and *The School for Scandal* there, and in 1779 *The Critic*. This completed his original work as dramatist. In 1780 he entered Parliament and continued there till 1812. He rose quickly to various important offices, and established a contemporary reputation as an orator which has never been surpassed, especially by his famous Begums speech of 1787, in which he supported the charges against the conduct of Warren Hastings to the Begums or princesses of Oude. The later years of his life were troubled by his debts, due chiefly to the compulsory rebuilding of Drury Lane in 1791 and its destruction by fire in 1809. He died in 1816.

I have been greatly indebted to Professor G. H. Nettleton's edition of *The Major Dramas* (Boston, 1906) and to Mr. W. H. Low's edition of *The Rivals* (Univ. Corr. Coll. Tutorial Series).

THE RIVALS

A COMEDY

AS PERFORMED AT THE

THEATRES-ROYAL

IN

DRURY LANE AND COVENT GARDEN

[The Sixth Edition. London : Printed for G. Wilkie,
No. 57 Paternoster Row. 1798.]

B

DRAMATIS PERSONAE

AS ORIGINALLY ACTED AT COVENT GARDEN THEATRE IN 1775.

MEN.

SIR ANTHONY ABSOLUTE .	Mr. Shuter.
CAPTAIN ABSOLUTE . .	Mr. Woodward.
FAULKLAND	Mr. Lewis.
ACRES	Mr. Quick.
SIR LUCIUS O'TRIGGER .	Mr. Clinch.
FAG	Mr. Lee Lewes.
DAVID	Mr. Dunstall.
COACHMAN	Mr. Fearon.

WOMEN.

MRS. MALAPROP. . . .	Mrs. Green.
LYDIA LANGUISH . . .	Miss Barsanti.
JULIA	Mrs. Bulkley.
LUCY	Mrs. Lessingham.

Maid, Boy, Servants, &c.

SCENE—*Bath.*

Time of Action, within One Day.

PROLOGUE

BY THE AUTHOR

SPOKEN BY MR. WOODWARD AND MR. QUICK

Enter SERJEANT-AT-LAW, *and* ATTORNEY *following,* **and**
giving a Paper.

Serj. What 's here—a vile cramp hand ! I cannot
    see
Without my spectacles.
    Att.   He means his fee.
Nay, Mr. Serjeant, good sir, try again.   [*Gives money.*
    Serj. The scrawl improves ! [*more*] Oh come, 'tis
        pretty plain.
Hey ! how 's this ?—Dibble !—sure it cannot be !
A poet's brief ! A poet and a fee !
    Att. Yea, sir !—tho' *you* without reward, I know,
Would gladly plead the Muse's cause—
    Serj.   So—so!
    Att. And if the fee offends—your wrath should fall
On me—
    Serj.   Dear Dibble, no offence at all—
    Att. Some sons of Phœbus—in the courts we meet,
    Serj. And fifty sons of Phœbus in the Fleet !
    Att. Nor pleads he worse, who with a decent sprig
Of bays—adorns his legal waste of wig.
    Serj. Full-bottomed heroes thus, on signs, unfurl
A leaf of laurel—in a grove of curl !
Yet tell your client, that, in adverse days,
This wig is warmer than a bush of bays.
    Att. Do you then, sir, my client's place supply,
Profuse of robe, and prodigal of tie——
Do you, with all those blushing powers of face,
And wonted bashful hesitating grace,
Rise in the court, and flourish on the case.   [*Exit.*

Serj. For practice then suppose—this brief will show
    it——
Me, Serjeant Woodward,—counsel for the poet.
Used to the ground—I know 'tis hard to deal
With this dread court, from whence there's no appeal;
No tricking here, to blunt the edge of law,
Or, damned in equity—escape by flaw :
But judgement given—your sentence must remain ;
—No writ of error lies—to Drury Lane !
    Yet when so kind you seem—'tis past dispute
We gain some favour, if not costs of suit.
No spleen is here ! I see no hoarded fury ;
—I think I never faced a milder jury !
Sad else our plight !—where frowns are transportation,
A hiss the gallows—and a groan, damnation !
But such the public candour, without fear
My client waives all right of challenge here.
No newsman from our session is dismissed,
Nor wit nor critic we scratch off the list ;
His faults can never hurt another's ease,
His crime at worst—a bad attempt to please :
Thus, all respecting, he appeals to all,
And by the general voice will stand or fall.

PROLOGUE

By the Author

SPOKEN ON THE TENTH NIGHT BY MRS. BULKLEY

GRANTED our cause, our suit and trial o'er,
The worthy serjeant need appear no more :
In pleasing I a different client choose,
He served the Poet—I would serve the Muse :
Like him, I'll try to merit your applause,
A female counsel in a female's cause.
   Look on this form [1]—where humour, quaint and sly,
Dimples the cheek, and points the beaming eye ;
Where gay invention seems to boast its wiles
In amorous hint, and half-triumphant smiles ;
While her light mask or covers satire's strokes,
Or hides the conscious blush her wit provokes.
—Look on her well—does she seem formed to teach ?
Should you expect to hear this lady—preach ?
Is grey experience suited to her youth ?
Do solemn sentiments become that mouth ?
Bid her be grave, those lips should rebel prove
To every theme that slanders mirth or love.
   Yet thus adorned with every graceful art
To charm the fancy and yet reach the heart——
Must we displace her ? And instead advance
The goddess of the woful countenance—
The sentimental Muse !—Her emblems view,
The Pilgrim's Progress, and a sprig of rue !
View her—too chaste to look like flesh and blood—
Primly portrayed on emblematic wood !
There fixed in usurpation should she stand,
She'll snatch the dagger from her sister's hand :
And having made her vot'ries weep a flood,
Good Heaven ! she'll end her comedies in blood—

       [1] Pointing to the figure of Comedy.

Bid Harry Woodward break poor Dunstall's crown !
Imprison Quick—and knock Ned Shuter down ;
While sad Barsanti—weeping o'er the scene—
Shall stab herself—or poison Mrs. Green.——

    Such dire encroachments to prevent in time,
Demands the critic's voice—the poet's rhyme.
Can our light scenes add strength to holy laws ?
Such puny patronage but hurts the cause :
Fair virtue scorns our feeble aid to ask ;
And moral truth disdains the trickster's mask.
For here their fav'rite stands [1], whose brow—severe
And sad—claims youth's respect, and pity's tear ;
Who—when oppressed by foes her worth creates—
Can point a poniard at the guilt she hates.

[1] Pointing to Tragedy.

EPILOGUE

By the Author

SPOKEN BY MRS. BULKLEY

LADIES, for you—I heard our poet say—
He'd try to coax some moral from his play :
' One moral 's plain'—cried I—'without more fuss ;
Man's social happiness all rests on us :
Thro' all the drama—whether damned or not—
Love gilds the scene, and women guide the plot.
From ev'ry rank, obedience is our due—
D'ye doubt ?—The world's great stage shall prove it
    true.'
    The Cit—well skilled to shun domestic strife—
Will sup abroad ;—but first—he'll ask his wife :
John Trot, his friend, for once will do the same,
But then—he'll just step home to tell his dame.
    The surly Squire—at noon resolves to rule,
And half the day—Zounds ! madam is a fool !
Convinced at night—the vanquished victor says,
Ah ! Kate ! you women have such coaxing ways !
    The jolly toper chides each tardy blade—
Till reeling Bacchus calls on Love for aid :
Then with each toast, he sees fair bumpers swim,
And kisses Chloe on the sparkling brim !
    Nay, I have heard that statesmen—great and wise—
Will sometimes counsel with a lady's eyes ;
The servile suitors—watch her various face,
She smiles preferment—or she frowns disgrace,
Curtsies a pension here—there nods a place.
    Nor with less awe, in scenes of humbler life,
Is viewed the mistress, or is heard the wife.
The poorest peasant of the poorest soil,
The child of poverty, and heir to toil—
Early from radiant Love's impartial light,
Steals one small spark, to cheer his world of night :

Dear spark !—that oft thro' winter's chilling woes,
Is all the warmth his little cottage knows :
The wand'ring tar—who, not for years, has pressed
The widowed partner of his day of rest,
On the cold deck—far from her arms removed—
Still hums the ditty which his Susan loved : .
And while around the cadence rude is blown,
The boatswain whistles in a softer tone.

  The soldier, fairly proud of wounds and toil,
Pants for the triumph of his Nancy's smile ;
But ere the battle, should he list her cries,
The lover trembles—and the hero dies !
That heart, by war and honour steeled to fear,
Droops on a sigh, and sickens at a tear !

  But ye more cautious—ye nice-judging few,
Who give to beauty only beauty's due,
Tho' friends to love—ye view with deep regret
Our conquests marred—and triumphs incomplete,
Till polished wit more lasting charms disclose,
And judgement fix the darts which beauty throws !
—In female breasts did sense and merit rule,
The lover's mind would ask no other school ;
Shamed into sense—the scholars of our eyes,
Our beaux from gallantry would soon be wise ;
Would gladly light, their homage to improve,
The lamp of Knowledge at the torch of Love !

THE RIVALS

ACT I

SCENE I.—*A Street in Bath.*

COACHMAN *crosses the Stage. Enter* FAG, *looking after him.*

Fag. What!—Thomas!—Sure 'tis he?—What!—Thomas!—Thomas!

Coach. Hey! Odds life!—Mr. Fag!—give us your hand, my old fellow servant.

Fag. Excuse my glove, Thomas!—I'm dev'lish glad to see you, my lad: why, my prince of charioteers, you look as hearty!—but who the deuce thought of seeing you in Bath?

Coach. Sure, Master, Madam Julia, Harry, Mrs. Kate, and the postilion be all come.

Fag. Indeed!

Coach. Aye! Master thought another fit of the gout was coming to make him a visit;—so he'd a mind to gi't the slip, and whip! we were all off at an hour's warning.

Fag. Aye, aye! hasty in everything, or it would not be Sir Anthony Absolute!

Coach. But tell us, Mr. Fag, how does young Master? Odd! Sir Anthony will stare to see the captain here!

Fag. I do not serve Captain Absolute now.

Coach. Why sure!

Fag. At present I am employ'd by Ensign Beverley.

Coach. I doubt, Mr. Fag, you ha'n't changed for the better.

Fag. I have not changed, Thomas.

Coach. No! why didn't you say you had left young master?

Fag. No.—Well, honest Thomas, I must puzzle you

no farther ;—briefly then—Captain Absolute and Ensign Beverley are one and the same person.

Coach. The devil they are !

Fag. So it is indeed, Thomas ; and the ensign-half of my master being on guard at present, the Captain has nothing to do with me.

Coach. So, so!—what, this is some freak, I warrant !—Do tell us, Mr. Fag, the meaning o't—you know I ha' trusted you.

Fag. You'll be secret, Thomas ?

Coach. As a coach-horse.

Fag. Why then the cause of all this is—Love—Love, Thomas, who (as you may get read to you) has been a masquerader ever since the days of Jupiter.

Coach. Aye, aye;—I guess'd there was a lady in the case :—but pray, why does your master pass only for Ensign ?—now if he had shamm'd General indeed——

Fag. Ah ! Thomas, there lies the mystery o' the matter.—Hark'ee, Thomas, my master is in love with a lady of a very singular taste : a lady who likes him better as a half-pay ensign, than if she knew he was son and heir to Sir Anthony Absolute, a baronet of three thousand a year.

Coach. That is an odd taste indeed !—but has she got the stuff, Mr. Fag ; is she rich, hey ?

Fag. Rich !—why, I believe she owns half the stocks !—Z—ds ! Thomas, she could pay the national debt as easily as I could my washerwoman !—She has a lap-dog that eats out of gold,—she feeds her parrot with small pearls,—and all her thread-papers are made of bank-notes !

Coach. Bravo !—faith !—Odd !—I warrant she has a set of thousands at least :—but does she draw kindly with the Captain ?

Fag. As fond as pigeons.

Coach. May one hear her name ?

Fag. Miss Lydia Languish.—But there is an old tough aunt in the way ;—though, by the by, she has never seen my master—for he got acquainted with Miss while on a visit in Gloucestershire.

Coach. Well—I wish they were once harnessed together in matrimony. — But pray, Mr. Fag, what kind of a place is this Bath ?—I ha' heard a deal of it—here 's a mort o' merrymaking—hey ?

Fag. Pretty well, Thomas, pretty well—'tis a good lounge ; in the morning we go to the pump-room (though neither my master nor I drink the waters) ; after breakfast we saunter on the Parades or play a game at billiards; at night we dance : but d—n the place, I'm tired of it ; their regular hours stupefy me—not a fiddle nor a card after eleven !—however, Mr. Faulkland's gentleman and I keep it up a little in private parties ;—I'll introduce you there, Thomas—you'll like him much.

Coach. Sure I know Mr. Du-Peign—you know his master is to marry Madam Julia.

Fag. I had forgot.—But, Thomas, you must polish a little—indeed you must——Here now—this wig !—what the devil do you do with a wig, Thomas ?—none of the London whips of any degree of *ton* wear wigs now.

Coach. More 's the pity ! more 's the pity, I say—Odd's life ! when I heard how the lawyers and doctors had took to their own hair, I thought how 'twould go next :—Odd rabbit it ! when the fashion had got foot on the Bar, I guess'd 'twould mount to the Box!—but 'tis all out of character, believe me, Mr. Fag : and look'ee, I'll never gi' up mine—the lawyers and doctors may do as they will.

Fag. Well, Thomas, we'll not quarrel about that.

Coach. Why, bless you, the gentlemen of they professions ben't all of a mind—for in our village now, thoff Jack Gauge the exciseman has ta'en to his carrots, there 's little Dick the farrier swears he'll never forsake his bob, tho' all the college should appear with their own heads !

Fag. Indeed ! well said, Dick ! but hold—mark ! mark ! Thomas.

Coach. Zooks ! 'tis the Captain.—Is that the lady with him ?

Fag. No! no! that is Madam Lucy—my master's mistress's maid.—They lodge at that house—but I must after him to tell him the news.

Coach. Odd! he 's giving her money!—well, Mr. Fag——

Fag. Good-bye, Thomas.—I have an appointment in Gyde's Porch this evening at eight; meet me there, and we'll make a little party.   [*Exeunt severally.*

SCENE II.—*A Dressing-room in* MRS. MALAPROP'S *Lodgings.*

LYDIA *sitting on a sofa, with a book in her hand.*— LUCY, *as just returned from a message.*

Lucy. Indeed, ma'am, I travers'd half the town in search of it: I don't believe there 's a circulating library in Bath I ha'n't been at.

Lyd. And could not you get *The Reward of Constancy* ?

Lucy. No, indeed, ma'am.

Lyd. Nor *The Fatal Connexion* ?

Lucy. No, indeed, ma'am.

Lyd. Nor *The Mistakes of the Heart* ?

Lucy. Ma'am, as ill luck would have it, Mr. Bull said Miss Sukey Saunter had just fetch'd it away.

Lyd. Heigh-ho!—Did you inquire for *The Delicate Distress* ?

Lucy. ——Or, *The Memoirs of Lady Woodford* ? Yes, indeed, ma'am. I asked everywhere for it; and I might have brought it from Mr. Frederick's, but Lady Slattern Lounger, who had just sent it home, had so soiled and dog's-ear'd it, it wa'n't fit for a Christian to read.

Lyd. Heigh-ho!—Yes, I always know when Lady Slattern has been before me. She has a most observing thumb; and I believe cherishes her nails for the convenience of making marginal notes.—Well, child, what *have* you brought me ?

Lucy. Oh! here, ma'am.

[*Taking books from under her cloak, and from her pockets.*

This is *The Gordian Knot,*—and this *Peregrine Pickle.* Here are *The Tears of Sensibility,* and *Humphrey Clinker.* This is *The Memoirs of a Lady of Quality, written by herself,* and here the second volume of *The Sentimental Journey.*

Lyd. Heigh-ho !—What are those books by the glass ?

Lucy. The great one is only *The Whole Duty of Man,* where I press a few blonds, ma'am.

Lyd. Very well—give me the sal volatile.

Lucy. Is it in a blue cover, ma'am ?

Lyd. My smelling bottle, you simpleton !

Lucy. Oh, the drops !—here, ma'am.

Lyd. Hold !—here 's some one coming—quick, see who it is——   [*Exit* LUCY.
Surely I heard my cousin Julia's voice !

Re-enter LUCY.

Lucy. Lud ! ma'am, here is Miss Melville.

Lyd. Is it possible !——

Enter JULIA.

Lyd. My dearest Julia, how delighted am I ! [*Embrace.*] How unexpected was this happiness !

Jul. True, Lydia—and our pleasure is the greater ;— but what has been the matter ?—you were denied to me at first !

Lyd. Ah, Julia, I have a thousand things to tell you !—but first inform me what has conjur'd you to Bath ?—Is Sir Anthony here ?

Jul. He is—we are arrived within this hour—and I suppose he will be here to wait on Mrs. Malaprop as soon as he is dressed.

Lyd. Then before we are interrupted, let me impart to you some of my distress !—I know your gentle nature will sympathize with me, though your prudence may condemn me !—My letters have informed you of my whole connexion with Beverley ;—but I have lost him, Julia !—my aunt has discovered our intercourse by a note she intercepted, and has confined me ever since ! Yet, would you believe it ? she has fallen absolutely in love with a tall Irish baronet she met one night since we have been here at Lady Macshuffle's rout.

Jul. You jest, Lydia!

Lyd. No, upon my word. She really carries on a kind of correspondence with him, under a feigned name though, till she chooses to be known to him;— but it is a Delia or a Celia, I assure you.

Jul. Then, surely, she is now more indulgent to her niece.

Lyd. Quite the contrary. Since she has discovered her own frailty she is become more suspicious of mine. Then I must inform you of another plague! That odious Acres is to be in Bath to-day; so that I protest I shall be teased out of all spirits!

Jul. Come, come, Lydia, hope for the best—Sir Anthony shall use his interest with Mrs. Malaprop.

Lyd. But you have not heard the worst. Unfortunately I had quarrelled with my poor Beverley, just before my aunt made the discovery, and I have not seen him since, to make it up.

Jul. What was his offence?

Lyd. Nothing at all! But, I don't know how it was, as often as we had been together, we had never had a quarrel, and, somehow, I was afraid he would never give me an opportunity. So, last Thursday, I wrote a letter to myself, to inform myself that Beverley was at that time paying his addresses to another woman. I signed it *your friend unknown,* showed it to Beverley, charged him with his falsehood, put myself in a violent passion, and vowed I'd never see him more.

Jul. And you let him depart so, and have not seen him since?

Lyd. 'Twas the next day my aunt found the matter out. I intended only to have teased him three days and a half, and now I've lost him for ever.

Jul. If he is as deserving and sincere as you have represented him to me, he will never give you up so. Yet consider, Lydia, you tell me he is but an ensign, and you have thirty thousand pounds!

Lyd. But you know I lose most of my fortune if
I marry without my aunt's consent, till of age ; and
that is what I have determined to do, ever since
I knew the penalty. Nor could I love the man who
would wish to wait a day for the alternative.

Jul. Nay, this is caprice !

Lyd. What, does Julia tax me with caprice ?   I
thought her lover Faulkland had inured her to it.

Jul. I do not love even *his* faults.

Lyd. But à propos—you have sent to him, I suppose ?

Jul. Not yet, upon my word—nor has he the least
idea of my being in Bath. Sir Anthony's resolution
was so sudden, I could not inform him of it.

Lyd. Well, Julia, you are your own mistress (though
under the protection of Sir Anthony), yet have you,
for this long year, been a slave to the caprice, the
whim, the jealousy of this ungrateful Faulkland, who
will ever delay assuming the right of a husband, while
you suffer him to be equally imperious as a lover.

Jul. Nay, you are wrong entirely. We were con-
tracted before my father's death. That, and some
consequent embarrassments, have delayed what I know
to be my Faulkland's most ardent wish. He is too
generous to trifle on such a point. And for his character, you wrong him there too. No, Lydia, he is too
proud, too noble to be jealous ; if he is captious, 'tis
without dissembling ; if fretful, without rudeness.
Unused to the fopperies of love, he is negligent of the
little duties expected from a lover—but being un-
hackneyed in the passion, his affection is ardent and
sincere ; and as it engrosses his whole soul, he expects
every thought and emotion of his mistress to move in
unison with his. Yet, though his pride calls for this
full return, his humility makes him undervalue those
qualities in him, which would entitle him to it ; and
not feeling why he should be loved to the degree he
wishes, he still suspects that he is not loved enough.
This temper, I must own, has cost me many unhappy
hours ; but I have learned to think myself his debtor,

for those imperfections which arise from the ardour of his attachment.

Lyd. Well, I cannot blame you for defending him. But tell me candidly, Julia, had he never saved your life, do you think you should have been attached to him as you are? Believe me, the rude blast that overset your boat was a prosperous gale of love to him.

Jul. Gratitude may have strengthened my attachment to Mr. Faulkland, but I loved him before he had preserved me; yet surely that alone were an obligation sufficient——

Lyd. Obligation!——Why a water-spaniel would have done as much! Well, I should never think of giving my heart to a man because he could swim!

Jul. Come, Lydia, you are too inconsiderate.

Lyd. Nay, I do but jest.—What's here?

Enter LUCY *in a hurry.*

Lucy. Oh, ma'am, here is Sir Anthony Absolute just come home with your aunt.

Lyd. They'll not come here.—Lucy, do you watch
[*Exit* LUCY.

Jul. Yet I must go. Sir Anthony does not know I am here, and if we meet, he'll detain me, to show me the town. I'll take another opportunity of paying my respects to Mrs. Malaprop, when she shall treat me, as long as she chooses, with her select words so ingeniously *misapplied*, without being *mispronounced*.

Re-enter LUCY.

Lucy. O Lud! ma'am, they are both coming upstairs.

Lyd. Well, I'll not detain you, coz.—Adieu, my dear Julia, I'm sure you are in haste to send to Faulkland.——There, through my room you'll find another staircase.

Jul. Adieu. [*Embrace.*]　　　　　[*Exit* JULIA.

Lyd. Here, my dear Lucy, hide these books. Quick, quick. Fling *Peregrine Pickle* under the toilet—throw *Roderick Random* into the closet—put *The Innocent*

Adultery into *The Whole Duty of Man*—thrust *Lord Aimworth* under the sofa—cram *Ovid* behind the bolster —there—put *The Man of Feeling* into your pocket— so, so, now lay *Mrs. Chapone* in sight, and leave *Fordyce's Sermons* open on the table.

Lucy. Oh, burn it, ma'am, the hairdresser has torn away as far as *Proper Pride.*

Lyd. Never mind—open at *Sobriety.* Fling me *Lord Chesterfield's Letters.*—Now for 'em.

Enter MRS. MALAPROP *and* SIR ANTHONY ABSOLUTE.

Mrs. Mal. There, Sir Anthony, there sits the deliberate simpleton, who wants to disgrace her family, and lavish herself on a fellow not worth a shilling.

Lyd. Madam, I thought you once——

Mrs. Mal. You thought, miss! I don't know any business you have to think at all. Thought does not become a young woman. But the point we would request of you is, that you will promise to forget this fellow—to illiterate him, I say, quite from your memory.

Lyd. Ah, madam! our memories are independent of our wills. It is not so easy to forget.

Mrs. Mal. But I say it is, miss; there is nothing on earth so easy as to *forget,* if a person chooses to set about it. I'm sure I have as much forgot your poor dear uncle, as if he had never existed—and I thought it my duty so to do; and let me tell you, Lydia, these violent memories don't become a young woman.

Sir Anth. Why, sure, she won't pretend to remember what she's ordered not!—aye, this comes of her reading!

Lyd. What crime, madam, have I committed to be treated thus?

Mrs. Mal. Now don't attempt to extirpate yourself from the matter; you know I have proof controvertible of it. But tell me, will you promise to do as you're bid? Will you take a husband of your friends' choosing?

Lyd. Madam, I must tell you plainly, that had I no

preference for any one else, the choice you have made would be my aversion.

Mrs. Mal. What business have you, miss, with *preference* and *aversion*? They don't become a young woman; and you ought to know, that as both always wear off, 'tis safest in matrimony to begin with a little *aversion.* I am sure I hated your poor dear uncle before marriage as if he'd been a black-a-moor—and yet, miss, you are sensible what a wife I made!—and when it pleased Heaven to release me from him, 'tis unknown what tears I shed! But suppose we were going to give you another choice, will you promise us to give up this Beverley?

Lyd. Could I belie my thoughts so far as to give that promise, my actions would certainly as far belie my words.

Mrs. Mal. Take yourself to your room. You are fit company for nothing but your own ill-humours.

Lyd. Willingly, ma'am—I cannot change for the worse.   [*Exit* LYDIA.

Mrs. Mal. There's a little intricate hussy for you!

Sir Anth. It is not to be wondered at, ma'am—all this is the natural consequence of teaching girls to read. Had I a thousand daughters, by Heaven! I'd as soon have them taught the black art as their alphabet!

Mrs. Mal. Nay, nay, Sir Anthony, you are an absolute misanthropy.

Sir Anth. In my way hither, Mrs. Malaprop, I observed your niece's maid coming forth from a circulating library! She had a book in each hand—they were half-bound volumes, with marble covers! From that moment I guessed how full of duty I should see her mistress!

Mrs. Mal. Those are vile places, indeed!

Sir Anth. Madam, a circulating library in a town is, as an ever-green tree of diabolical knowledge! It blossoms through the year! And depend on it, Mrs. Malaprop, that they who are so fond of handling the leaves, will long for the fruit at last.

Mrs. Mal. Fie, fie, Sir Anthony, you surely speak laconically.

Sir Anth. Why, Mrs. Malaprop, in moderation, now, what would you have a woman know ?

Mrs. Mal. Observe me, Sir Anthony. I would by no means wish a daughter of mine to be a progeny of learning ; I don't think so much learning becomes a young woman ; for instance—I would never let her meddle with Greek, or Hebrew, or Algebra, or Simony, or Fluxions, or Paradoxes, or such inflammatory branches of learning—neither would it be necessary for her to handle any of your mathematical, astronomical, diabolical instruments :—But, Sir Anthony, I would send her, at nine years old, to a boarding-school, in order to learn a little ingenuity and artifice. Then, sir, she should have a supercilious knowledge in accounts ;—and as she grew up, I would have her instructed in geometry, that she might know something of the contagious countries ;—but above all, Sir Anthony, she should be mistress of orthodoxy, that she might not misspell, and mispronounce words so shamefully as girls usually do ; and likewise that she might reprehend the true meaning of what she is saying. This, Sir Anthony, is what I would have a woman know ;—and I don't think there is a superstitious article in it.

Sir Anth. Well, well, Mrs. Malaprop, I will dispute the point no further with you ; though I must confess that you are a truly moderate and polite arguer, for almost every third word you say is on my side of the question. But, Mrs. Malaprop, to the more important point in debate—you say, you have no objection to my proposal ?

Mrs. Mal. None, I assure you. I am under no positive engagement with Mr. Acres, and as Lydia is so obstinate against him, perhaps your son may have better success.

Sir Anth. Well, madam, I will write for the boy directly. He knows not a syllable of this yet, though I have for some time had the proposal in my head. He is at present with his regiment.

Mrs. Mal. We have never seen your son, Sir Anthony; but I hope no objection on his side.

Sir Anth. Objection! let him object if he dare!—No, no, Mrs. Malaprop, Jack knows that the least demur puts me in a frenzy directly. My process was always very simple: in their younger days 'twas 'Jack, do this'; —if he demurred, I knocked him down—and if he grumbled at that, I always sent him out of the room.

Mrs. Mal. Aye, and the properest way, o' my conscience! nothing is so conciliating to young people as severity.—Well, Sir Anthony, I shall give Mr. Acres his discharge, and prepare Lydia to receive your son's invocations;—and I hope you will represent *her* to the Captain as an object not altogether illegible.

Sir Anth. Madam, I will handle the subject prudently.—Well, I must leave you; and let me beg you, Mrs. Malaprop, to enforce this matter roundly to the girl;—take my advice—keep a tight hand; if she rejects this proposal—clap her under lock and key; and if you were just to let the servants forget to bring her dinner for three or four days, you can't conceive how she'd come about.   [*Exit* SIR ANTHONY.

Mrs. Mal. Well, at any rate I shall be glad to get her from under my intuition. She has somehow discovered my partiality for Sir Lucius O'Trigger—sure, Lucy can't have betrayed me! No, the girl is such a simpleton, I should have made her confess it.—Lucy! Lucy! [*calls.*] Had she been one of your artificial ones, I should never have trusted her.

Enter LUCY.

Lucy. Did you call, ma'am?

Mrs. Mal. Yes, girl.—Did you see Sir Lucius while you was out?

Lucy. No, indeed, ma'am, not a glimpse of him.

Mrs. Mal. You are sure, Lucy, that you never mentioned——

Lucy. O Gemini! I'd sooner cut my tongue out.

Mrs. Mal. Well, don't let your simplicity be imposed on.

Lucy. No, ma'am.

Mrs. Mal. So, come to me presently, and I'll give you another letter to Sir Lucius; but mind, Lucy— if ever you betray what you are intrusted with (unless it be other people's secrets to me) you forfeit my malevolence for ever; and your being a simpleton shall be no excuse for your locality.   [*Exit* MRS. MAL.

Lucy. Ha! ha! ha!—So, my dear *simplicity*, let me give you a little respite—[*altering her manner*].— Let girls in my station be as fond as they please of appearing expert, and knowing in their trusts; commend me to a mask of silliness, and a pair of sharp eyes for my own interest under it!—Let me see to what account have I turned my simplicity lately.   [*Looks at a paper.*]   For *abetting Miss Lydia Languish in a design of running away with an Ensign !—in money— sundry times—twelve pound twelve—gowns, five—hats, ruffles, caps,* &c., &c.—*numberless ! From the said Ensign, within this last month, six guineas and a half.* About a quarter's pay !—Item, *from Mrs. Malaprop, for betraying the young people to her*—when I found matters were likely to be discovered—*two guineas, and a black padusoy.* Item, *from Mr. Acres, for carrying divers letters*—which I never delivered—*two guineas, and a pair of buckles.* Item, *from Sir Lucius O'Trigger —three crowns—two gold pocket-pieces—and a silver snuffbox !* Well done, *simplicity* !—yet I was forced to make my Hibernian believe that he was corresponding, not with the aunt, but with the niece : for though not over-rich, I found he had too much pride and delicacy to sacrifice the feelings of a gentleman to the necessities of his fortune.   [*Exit.*

ACT II

SCENE I.—CAPTAIN ABSOLUTE'S *Lodgings.*

CAPTAIN ABSOLUTE *and* FAG.

Fag. Sir, while I was there Sir Anthony came in : I told him, you had sent me to inquire after his health, and to know if he was at leisure to see you.

Abs. And what did he say, on hearing I was at Bath ?

Fag. Sir, in my life I never saw an elderly gentleman more astonished ! He started back two or three paces, rapped out a dozen interjectural oaths, and asked what the devil had brought you here ?

Abs. Well, sir, and what did you say ?

Fag. Oh, I lied, sir—I forget the precise lie ; but you may depend on't, he got no truth from me. Yet, with submission, for fear of blunders in future, I should be glad to fix what *has* brought us to Bath : in order that we may lie a little consistently. Sir Anthony's servants were curious, sir, very curious indeed.

Abs. You have said nothing to them—— ?

Fag. Oh, not a word, sir—not a word. Mr. Thomas, indeed, the coachman (whom I take to be the discreetest of whips)——

Abs. 'Sdeath!—you rascal! you have not trusted him!

Fag. Oh, *no*, sir—no—no—not a syllable, upon my veracity ! He was, indeed, a little inquisitive ; but I was sly, sir—devilish sly! My master (said I), honest Thomas (you know, sir, one says *honest* to one's inferiors), is come to Bath to recruit—yes, sir—I said *to recruit*—and whether for men, money, or constitution, you know, sir, is nothing to him, nor any one else.

Abs. Well—*recruit* will do—let it be so——

Fag. Oh, sir, recruit will do surprisingly—indeed, to give the thing an air, I told Thomas that your honour had already enlisted five disbanded chairmen, seven minority waiters, and thirteen billiard-markers.

Abs. You blockhead, never say more than is necessary.

Fag. I beg pardon, sir—I beg pardon—but, with submission, a lie is nothing unless one supports it. Sir, whenever I draw on my invention for a good current lie, I always forge endorsements as well as the bill.

Abs. Well, take care you don't hurt your credit, by offering too much security.—Is Mr. Faulkland returned ?

Fag. He is above, sir, changing his dress.

Abs. Can you tell whether he has been informed of Sir Anthony's and Miss Melville's arrival ?

Fag. I fancy not, sir ; he has seen no one since he came in, but his gentleman, who was with him at Bristol.—I think, sir, I hear Mr. Faulkland coming down——

Abs. Go, tell him I am here.

Fag. Yes, sir [*going*]—I beg pardon, sir, but should Sir Anthony call, you will do me the favour to remember that we are *recruiting*, if you please.

Abs. Well, well.

Fag. And in tenderness to my character, if your honour could bring in the chairmen and waiters, I should esteem it as an obligation ; for though I never scruple a lie to serve my master, yet it hurts one's conscience to be found out.   [*Exit.*

Abs. Now for my whimsical friend—if he does not know that his mistress is here, I'll tease him a little before I tell him.——

Enter FAULKLAND.

Faulkland, you're welcome to Bath again ; you are punctual in your return.

Faulk. Yes ; I had nothing to detain me, when I had finished the business I went on. Well, what news since I left you ? How stand matters between you and Lydia ?

Abs. Faith, much as they were ; I have not seen her since our quarrel ; however, I expect to be recalled every hour.

Faulk. Why don't you persuade her to go off with you at once ?

Abs. What, and lose two-thirds of her fortune ? You forget that, my friend. No, no, I could have brought her to that long ago

Faulk. Nay, then, you trifle too long—if you are sure of *her*, propose to the aunt *in your own character*, and write to Sir Anthony for his consent.

Abs. Softly, softly; for though I am convinced my little Lydia would elope with me as Ensign Beverley, yet am I by no means certain that she would take me with the impediment of our friends' consent, a regular humdrum wedding, and the reversion of a good fortune on my side : no, no ; I must prepare her gradually for the discovery, and make myself necessary to her, before I risk it.—Well, but Faulkland, you'll dine with us to-day at the hotel ?

Faulk. Indeed I cannot ; I am not in spirits to be of such a party.

Abs. By heavens ! I shall forswear your company. You are the most teasing, captious, incorrigible lover! Do love like a man!

Faulk. I own I am unfit for company.

Abs. Am not *I* a lover ; aye, and a romantic one too ? Yet do I carry everywhere with me such a confounded farrago of doubts, fears, hopes, wishes, and all the flimsy furniture of a country miss's brain ?

Faulk. Ah ! Jack, your heart and soul are not, like mine, fixed immutably on one only object. You throw for a large stake, but losing—you could stake, and throw again : but I have set my sum of happiness on this cast, and not to succeed were to be stript of all.

Abs. But, for Heaven's sake ! what grounds for apprehension can your whimsical brain conjure up at present ?

Faulk. What grounds for apprehension, did you say ? Heavens ! are there not a thousand ! I fear for her spirits—her health—her life! My absence may fret her ; her anxiety for my return, her fears for me, may oppress her gentle temper. And for her health, does not every hour bring me cause to be alarmed ? If it rains, some shower may even then have chilled her delicate frame ! If the wind be keen, some rude blast may have affected her ! The heat of noon, the dews of the evening, may endanger the life of her, for whom only I value mine. O Jack, when delicate and feeling souls are separated, there is not a feature in the sky, not a movement of the elements, not an aspiration of the breeze, but hints some cause for a lover's apprehension!

Abs. Aye, but we may choose whether we will take the hint or not.—So then, Faulkland, if you were convinced that Julia were well and in spirits, you would be entirely content?

Faulk. I should be happy beyond measure—I am anxious only for that.

Abs. Then to cure your anxiety at once—Miss Melville is in perfect health, and is at this moment in Bath.

Faulk. Nay, Jack—don't trifle with me.

Abs. She is arrived here with my father within this hour.

Faulk. Can you be serious?

Abs. I thought you knew Sir Anthony better than to be surprised at a sudden whim of this kind. Seriously then, it is as I tell you—upon my honour.

Faulk. My dear friend!—Hollo, Du-Peigne! my hat. —My dear Jack—now nothing on earth can give me a moment's uneasiness.

Enter FAG.

Fag. Sir, Mr. Acres, just arrived, is below.

Abs. Stay, Faulkland, this Acres lives within a mile of Sir Anthony, and he shall tell you how your mistress has been ever since you left her.—Fag, show the gentleman up.   [*Exit* FAG.

Faulk. What, is he much acquainted in the family?

Abs. Oh, very intimate: I insist on your not going: besides, his character will divert you.

Faulk. Well, I should like to ask him a few questions.

Abs. He is likewise a rival of mine—that is of my other self's, for he does not think his friend Captain Absolute ever saw the lady in question; and it is ridiculous enough to hear him complain to me of one Beverley, a concealed skulking rival, who——

Faulk. Hush ! He 's here.

Enter ACRES.

Acres. Hah ! my dear friend, noble captain, and honest Jack, how do'st thou ? just arrived, faith, as you see.—Sir, your humble servant. Warm work on the roads, Jack.—Odds whips and wheels ! I've travelled like a comet, with a tail of dust all the way as long as the Mall.

Abs. Ah ! Bob, you are indeed an eccentric planet, but we know your attraction hither.—Give me leave to introduce Mr. Faulkland to you ; Mr. Faulkland, Mr. Acres.

Acres. Sir, I am most heartily glad to see you : sir, I solicit your connexions.—Hey, Jack—what, this is Mr. Faulkland, who——

Abs. Aye, Bob, Miss Melville's Mr. Faulkland.

Acres. Odso ! she and your father can be but just arrived before me—I suppose you have seen them. Ah ! Mr. Faulkland, you are indeed a happy man.

Faulk. I have not seen Miss Melville yet, sir ; I hope she enjoyed full health and spirits in Devonshire ?

Acres. Never knew her better in my life, sir—never better. Odds blushes and blooms ! she has been as healthy as the German Spa.

Faulk. Indeed ! I did hear that she had been a little indisposed.

Acres. False, false, sir—only said to vex you : quite the reverse, I assure you.

Faulk. There, Jack, you see she has the advantage of me ; I had almost fretted myself ill.

Abs. Now are you angry with your mistress for not having been sick ?

Faulk. No, no, you misunderstand me : yet surely a little trifling indisposition is not an unnatural consequence of absence from those we love. Now confess —isn't there something unkind in this violent, robust, unfeeling health ?

Abs. Oh, it was very unkind of her to be well in your absence, to be sure !

Acres. Good apartments, Jack.

Faulk. Well, sir, but you was saying that Miss Melville has been so *exceedingly* well—what then, she has been merry and gay, I suppose ?   Always in spirits—hey ?

Acres. Merry, odds crickets ! she has been the belle and spirit of the company wherever she has been— so lively and entertaining ! so full of wit and humour !

Faulk. There, Jack, there.—Oh, by my soul ! there is an innate levity in woman that nothing can overcome.   What ! happy, and I away !

Abs. Have done : how foolish this is ! just now you were only apprehensive for your mistress's *spirits.*

Faulk. Why, Jack, have I been the joy and spirit of the company ?

Abs. No, indeed, you have not.

Faulk. Have I been lively and entertaining ?

Abs. Oh, upon my word, I acquit you.

Faulk. Have I been full of wit and humour ?

Abs. No, faith, to do you justice, you have been confoundedly stupid indeed.

Acres. What 's the matter with the gentleman ?

Abs. He is only expressing his great satisfaction at hearing that Julia has been so well and happy—that 's all—hey, Faulkland ?

Faulk. Oh ! I am rejoiced to hear it—yes, yes, she has a *happy* disposition !

Acres. That she has, indeed: then she is so accomplished—so sweet a voice—so expert at her harpsichord—such a mistress of flat and sharp, squallante, rumblante, and quiverante !—there was this time month —odds minnums and crotchets ! how she did chirrup at Mrs. Piano's concert.

Faulk. There again, what say you to this ? you see she has been all mirth and song—not a thought of me !

Abs. Pho ! man, is not ' music the food of love ' ?

Faulk. Well, well, it may be so.—Pray, Mr. ——, what 's his d—d name !—Do you remember what songs Miss Melville sung ?

Acres. Not I, indeed.

Abs. Stay now, they were some pretty, melancholy purling-stream airs, I warrant ; perhaps you may recollect ; did she sing *When absent from my soul's delight ?*

Acres. No, that wa'n't it.

Abs. Or, *Go, gentle gales ! Go, gentle gales !* [*Sings.*

Acres. Oh, no ! nothing like it. Odds ! now I recollect one of them—*My heart's my own, my will is free.*   [*Sings.*

Faulk. Fool ! fool that I am ! to fix all my happiness on such a trifler ! 'Sdeath ! to make herself the pipe and ballad-monger of a circle ! to soothe her light heart with catches and glees ! What can you say to this, sir ?

Abs. Why, that I should be glad to hear my mistress had been so merry, sir.

Faulk. Nay, nay, nay—I'm not sorry that she has been happy—no, no, I am glad of that—I would not have had her sad or sick ; yet surely a sympathetic heart would have shown itself even in the choice of a song—she might have been temperately healthy, and somehow, plaintively gay ; but she has been dancing too, I doubt not !

Acres. What does the gentleman say about dancing ?

Abs. He says the lady we speak of dances as well as she sings.

Acres. Aye, truly, does she—there was at our last race ball——

Faulk. Hell and the devil ! There ! there—I told you so ! I told you so ! Oh ! she thrives in my absence ! Dancing ! but her whole feelings have been in opposition with mine ; I have been anxious, silent, pensive, sedentary—my days have been hours of care, my nights of watchfulness. She has been all health ! spirit ! laugh ! song ! dance ! Oh ! d—ned, d—ned levity !

Abs. For Heaven's sake, Faulkland, don't expose yourself so. Suppose she has danced, what then ? does not the ceremony of society often oblige——

Faulk. Well, well, I'll contain myself—perhaps as
you say—for form sake. What, Mr. Acres, you were
praising Miss Melville's manner of dancing a minuet—
hey ?

Acres. Oh, I dare ensure her for that—but what
I was going to speak of was her country dancing : odds
swimmings ! she has such an air with her !

Faulk. Now disappointment on her !—defend this,
Absolute ; why don't you defend this ? Country-
dances ! jigs and reels ! am I to blame now ? A
minuet I could have forgiven—I should not have
minded that—I say I should not have regarded a
minuet—but country-dances ! Z—ds ! had she made
one in a cotillion—I believe I could have forgiven even
that—but to be monkey-led for a night !—to run the
gauntlet through a string of amorous palming puppies
—to show paces like a managed filly ! Oh Jack, there
never can be but *one* man in the world, whom a truly
modest and delicate woman ought to pair with in a
country-dance ; and even then the rest of the couples
should be her great uncles and aunts !

Abs. Aye, to be sure ! grandfathers and grand-
mothers !

Faulk. If there be but one vicious mind in the set,
'twill spread like a contagion—the action of their pulse
beats to the lascivious movement of the jig—their
quivering, warm-breathed sighs impregnate the very
air—the atmosphere becomes electrical to love, and
each amorous spark darts through every link of the
chain ! I must leave you—I own I am somewhat
flurried—and that confounded looby has perceived it.
　　　　　　　　　　　　　　　　　　　　　　　[*Going.*

Abs. Nay, but stay, Faulkland, and thank Mr. Acres
for his good news.

Faulk. D—n his news !　　　　　　[*Exit* FAULKLAND.

Abs. Ha ! ha ! ha ! poor Faulkland five minutes
since—' nothing on earth could give him a moment's
uneasiness ! '

Acres. The gentleman wa'n't angry at my praising
his mistress, was he ?

Abs. A little jealous, I believe, Bob.

Acres. You don't say so ? Ha ! ha ! jealous of me —that 's a good joke.

Abs. There 's nothing strange in that, Bob ; let me tell you, that sprightly grace and insinuating manner of yours will do some mischief among the girls here.

Acres. Ah ! you joke—ha ! ha ! mischief—ha ! ha ! but you know I am not my own property, my dear Lydia has forestalled me. She could never abide me in the country, because I used to dress so badly—but odds frogs and tambours ! I shan't take matters so here, now ancient madam has no voice in it—I'll make my old clothes know who 's master : I shall straightway cashier the hunting-frock, and render my leather breeches incapable. My hair has been in train-ing some time.

Abs. Indeed !

Acres. Aye, and thoff the side curls are a little restive, my hind-part takes it very kindly.

Abs. Oh, you'll polish, I doubt not.

Acres. Absolutely I propose so—then if I can find out this Ensign Beverley, odds triggers and flints ! I'll make him know the difference o't.

Abs. Spoke like a man—but pray, Bob, I observe you have got an odd kind of a new method of swearing——

Acres. Ha ! ha ! you've taken notice of it—'tis genteel, isn't it ? I didn't invent it myself though ; but a commander in our militia—a great scholar, I assure you—says that there is no meaning in the common oaths, and that nothing but their antiquity makes them respectable ; because, he says, the ancients would never stick to an oath or two, but would say, by Jove ! or by Bacchus ! or by Mars ! or by Venus ! or by Pallas ! according to the sentiment—so that to swear with propriety, says my little major, the 'oath should be an echo to the sense '; and this we call the *oath referential*, or *sentimental swearing*—ha ! ha ! ha ! 'tis genteel, isn't it ?

Abs. Very genteel, and very new indeed—and I dare say will supplant all other figures of imprecation.

Acres. Aye, aye, the best terms will grow obsolete. Damns have had their day.

Enter FAG.

Fag. Sir, there is a gentleman below desires to see you. Shall I show him into the parlour ?

Abs. Aye, you may.

Acres. Well, I must be gone——

Abs. Stay ; who is it, Fag ?

Fag. Your father, sir.

Abs. You puppy, why didn't you show him up directly ? [*Exit* FAG.

Acres. You have business with Sir Anthony. I expect a message from Mrs. Malaprop at my lodgings. I have sent also to my dear friend, Sir Lucius O'Trigger. Adieu, Jack, we must meet at night, when you shall give me a dozen bumpers to little Lydia.

Abs. That I will with all my heart. [*Exit* ACRES. Now for a parental lecture. I hope he has heard nothing of the business that has brought me here. I wish the gout had held him fast in Devonshire, with all my soul !

Enter SIR ANTHONY.

Sir, I am delighted to see you here ; and looking so well ! your sudden arrival at Bath made me apprehensive for your health.

Sir Anth. Very apprehensive, I dare say, Jack. What, you are recruiting here, hey ?

Abs. Yes, sir, I am on duty.

Sir Anth. Well, Jack, I am glad to see you, though I did not expect it, for I was going to write to you on a little matter of business. Jack, I have been considering that I grow old and infirm, and shall probably not trouble you long.

Abs. Pardon me, sir, I never saw you look more strong and hearty ; and I pray frequently that you may continue so.

Sir Anth. I hope your prayers may be heard with all my heart Well then, Jack, I have been considering that I am so strong and hearty, I may continue to plague you a long time. Now, Jack, I am sensible that the income of your commission, and what I have hitherto allowed you, is but a small pittance for a lad of your spirit.

Abs. Sir, you are very good.

Sir Anth. And it is my wish, while yet I live, to have my boy make some figure in the world. I have resolved, therefore, to fix you at once in a noble independence.

Abs. Sir, your kindness overpowers me—such generosity makes the gratitude of reason more lively than the sensations even of filial affection.

Sir Anth. I am glad you are so sensible of my attention—and you shall be master of a large estate in a few weeks.

Abs. Let my future life, sir, speak my gratitude; I cannot express the sense I have of your munificence. Yet, sir, I presume you would not wish me to quit the army?

Sir Anth. Oh, that shall be as your wife chooses.

Abs. My wife, sir!

Sir Anth. Aye, aye, settle that between you—settle that between you.

Abs. A *wife*, sir, did you say?

Sir Anth. Aye, a wife—why, did not I mention her before?

Abs. Not a word of her, sir.

Sir Anth. Oddso! I mustn't forget *her* though. Yes, Jack, the independence I was talking of is by a marriage—the fortune is saddled with a wife—but I suppose that makes no difference.

Abs. Sir! sir!—you amaze me!

Sir Anth. Why, what the devil's the matter with the fool? Just now you were all gratitude and duty.

Abs. I was, sir—you talked to me of independence and a fortune, but not a word of a wife.

Sir Anth. Why, what difference does that make! Odds life, sir! if you have the estate, you must take it with the live stock on it, as it stands.

Abs. If my happiness is to be the price, I must beg leave to decline the purchase. Pray, sir, who is the lady ?

Sir Anth. What's that to you, sir ? Come, give me your promise to love, and to marry her directly.

Abs. Sure, sir, this is not very reasonable, to summon my affections for a lady I know nothing of !

Sir Anth. I am sure, sir, 'tis more unreasonable in you to *object* to a lady you know nothing of.

Abs. Then, sir, I must tell you plainly, that my inclinations are fixed on another—my heart is engaged to an angel.

Sir Anth. Then pray let it send an excuse. It is very sorry—but *business* prevents its waiting on her.

Abs. But my vows are pledged to her.

Sir Anth. Let her foreclose, Jack ; let her foreclose ; they are not worth redeeming ; besides, you have the angel's vows in exchange, I suppose ; so there can be no loss there.

Abs. You must excuse me, sir, if I tell you, once for all, that in this point I cannot obey you.

Sir Anth. Hark'ee, Jack ; I have heard you for some time with patience—I have been cool—quite cool ; but take care—you know I am compliance itself—when I am not thwarted ; no one more easily led—when I have my own way ; but don't put me in a frenzy.

Abs. Sir, I must repeat it—in this I cannot obey you.

Sir Anth. Now, d—n me ! if ever I call you *Jack* again while I live !

Abs. Nay, sir, but hear me.

Sir Anth. Sir, I won't hear a word—not a word ! not one word ! so give me your promise by a nod—and I'll tell you what, Jack—I mean, you dog—if you don't, by——

Abs. What, sir, promise to link myself to some mass of ugliness ! to——

Sir Anth. Z—ds ! sirrah ! the lady shall be as ugly as I choose : she shall have a hump on each shoulder ;

D

she shall be as crooked as the Crescent ; her one eye
shall roll like the bull's in Cox's Museum ; she shall
have a skin like a mummy, and the beard of a Jew—
she shall be all this, sirrah !—yet I will make you
ogle her all day, and sit up all night to write sonnets
on her beauty.

Abs. This is reason and moderation indeed !

Sir Anth. None of your sneering, puppy ! no grinning,
jackanapes !

Abs. Indeed, sir, I never was in a worse humour for
mirth in my life.

Sir Anth. 'Tis false, sir, I know you are laughing
in your sleeve ; I know you'll grin when I am gone,
sirrah !

Abs. Sir, I hope I know my duty better.

Sir Anth. None of your passion, sir ! none of your
violence, if you please.   It won't do with me, I promise you.

Abs. Indeed, sir, I never was cooler in my life.

Sir Anth. 'Tis a confounded lie !   I know you are
in a passion in your heart ; I know you are, you hypo-
critical young dog ! but it won't do.

Abs. Nay, sir, upon my word.

Sir Anth. So you will fly out ! can't you be cool,
like me ?   What the devil good can passion do !
Passion is of no service, you impudent, insolent, over-
bearing reprobate !   There, you sneer again !—don't
provoke me !—but you rely upon the mildness of my
temper—you do, you dog ! you play upon the meek-
ness of my disposition !   Yet take care—the patience
of a saint may be overcome at last !—but mark ! I give
you six hours and a half to consider of this : if you then
agree, without any condition, to do everything on
earth that I choose, why—confound you ! I may in
time forgive you.   If not, z—ds ! don't enter the same
hemisphere with me ! don't dare to breathe the same
air, or use the same light with me ; but get an atmosphere and a sun of your own !   I'll strip you of your
commission ;   I'll lodge a five-and-threepence in the
hands of trustees, and you shall live on the interest.

I'll disown you, I'll disinherit you, I'll unget you!
and d—n me! if ever I call you Jack again!

[*Exit* SIR ANTHONY.

ABSOLUTE *solus.*

Abs. Mild, gentle, considerate father—I kiss your
hands. What a tender method of giving his opinion
in these matters Sir Anthony has! I dare not trust
him with the truth. I wonder what old wealthy hag
it is that he wants to bestow on me!—yet he married
himself for love! and was in his youth a bold intriguer
and a gay companion!

Enter FAG.

Fag. Assuredly, sir, your father is wroth to a degree;
he comes downstairs eight or ten steps at a time—
muttering, growling, and thumping the banisters all
the way: I, and the cook's dog, stand bowing at the
door—rap! he gives me a stroke on the head with his
cane; bids me carry that to my master, then kicking
the poor turnspit into the area, d—ns us all for
a puppy triumvirate! Upon my credit, sir, were I in
your place, and found my father such very bad company, I should certainly drop his acquaintance.

Abs. Cease your impertinence, sir, at present. Did
you come in for nothing more?—Stand out of the way!

[*Pushes him aside, and exit.*

FAG *solus.*

Fag. So! Sir Anthony trims my master: he is
afraid to reply to his father—then vents his spleen on
poor Fag! When one is vexed by one person, to
revenge oneself on another, who happens to come in
the way, is the vilest injustice! Ah! it shows the
worst temper—the basest——

Enter ERRAND BOY.

Boy. Mr. Fag! Mr. Fag! your master calls you.

Fag. Well! you little dirty puppy, you need not
bawl so!—The meanest disposition! the——

Boy. Quick, quick, Mr. Fag

Fag. Quick! quick! you impudent jackanapes! am I to be commanded by you too? you little, impertinent, insolent, kitchen-bred——

[*Exit kicking and beating him.*

SCENE II.—*The North Parade.*

Enter LUCY.

Lucy. So—I shall have another rival to add to my mistress's list—Captain Absolute. However, I shall not enter his name till my purse has received notice in form. Poor Acres is dismissed! Well, I have done him a last friendly office, in letting him know that Beverley was here before him. Sir Lucius is generally more punctual, when he expects to hear from his *dear Dalia,* as he calls her: I wonder he's not here! I have a little scruple of conscience from this deceit; though I should not be paid so well if my hero knew that *Delia* was near fifty, and her own mistress.

Enter SIR LUCIUS O'TRIGGER.

Sir Luc. Ha! my little ambassadress—upon my conscience I have been looking for you; I have been on the South Parade this half hour.

Lucy. [*Speaking simply.*] O Gemini! and I have been waiting for your worship here on the North.

Sir Luc. Faith!—may-be, that was the reason we did not meet; and it is very comical too, how you could go out and I not see you—for I was only taking a nap at the Parade Coffee-house, and I chose the *window* on purpose that I might not miss you.

Lucy. My stars! Now I'd wager a sixpence I went by while you were asleep.

Sir Luc. Sure enough it must have been so—and I never dreamt it was so late, till I waked. Well, but my little girl, have you got nothing for me?

Lucy. Yes, but I have—I've got a letter for you in my pocket.

Sir Luc. Oh, faith! I guessed you weren't come empty-handed—well—let me see what the dear creature says.

Lucy. There, Sir Lucius. [*Gives him a letter.*]

Sir Luc. [Reads.] ' *Sir—there is often a sudden incentive impulse in love, that has a greater induction than years of domestic combination : such was the commotion I felt at the first superfluous view of Sir Lucius O'Trigger.*' Very pretty, upon my word. ' *Female punctuation forbids me to say more ; yet let me add, that it will give me joy infallible to find Sir Lucius worthy the last criterion of my affections.*   DELIA.'
Upon my conscience, Lucy, your lady is a great mistress of language. Faith, she's quite the queen of the dictionary !—for the devil a word dare refuse coming at her call—though one would think it was quite out of hearing.

Lucy. Aye, sir, a lady of her experience.

Sir Luc. Experience ? what, at seventeen ?

Lucy. Oh, true, sir—but then she reads so—my stars ! how she will read off hand !

Sir Luc. Faith, she must be very deep read to write this way—though she is rather an arbitrary writer too, for here are a great many poor words pressed into the service of this note, that would get their *habeas corpus* from any court in Christendom.

Lucy. Ah ! Sir Lucius, if you were to hear how she talks of you!

Sir Luc. Oh, tell her, I'll make her the best husband in the world, and Lady O'Trigger into the bargain ! But we must get the old gentlewoman's consent—and do everything fairly.

Lucy. Nay, Sir Lucius, I thought you wa'n't rich enough to be so nice !

Sir Luc. Upon my word, young woman, you have hit it : I am so poor, that I can't afford to do a dirty action. If I did not want money, I'd steal your mistress and her fortune with a great deal of pleasure. However, my pretty girl, [*gives her money*] here's a little something to buy you a ribbon ; and meet me in the evening, and I'll give you an answer to this. So, hussy, take a kiss beforehand, to put you in mind.
                                        [*Kisses her.*]

Lucy. O Lud! Sir Lucius—I never seed such a gemman! My lady won't like you if you're so impudent.

Sir Luc. Faith, she will, Lucy—that same—pho! what's the name of it?—*modesty!*—is a quality in a lover more praised by the women than liked; so, if your mistress asks you whether Sir Lucius ever gave you a kiss, tell her fifty, my dear.

Lucy. What, would you have me tell her a lie?

Sir Luc. Ah, then, you baggage! I'll make it a truth presently.

Lucy. For shame, now; here is some one coming.

Sir Luc. Oh, faith, I'll quiet your conscience!

[*Sees* FAG. *Exit, humming a tune.*

Enter FAG.

Fag. So, so, madam. I humbly beg pardon.

Lucy. O Lud! now, Mr. Fag—you flurry one so.

Fag. Come, come, Lucy, here's no one by—so a little less simplicity, with a grain or two more sincerity, if you please. You play false with us, madam. I saw you give the baronet a letter. My master shall know this—and if he don't call him out, I will.

Lucy. Ha! ha! ha! you gentlemen's gentlemen are so hasty. That letter was from Mrs. Malaprop, simpleton. She is taken with Sir Lucius's address.

Fag. How! what tastes some people have! Why, I suppose I have walked by her window a hundred times. But what says our young lady? Any message to my master?

Lucy. Sad news! Mr. Fag. A worse rival than Acres! Sir Anthony Absolute has proposed his son.

Fag. What, Captain Absolute?

Lucy. Even so—I overheard it all.

Fag. Ha! ha! ha! very good, faith. Good-bye, Lucy, I must away with this news.

Lucy. Well—you may laugh—but it is true, I assure you. [*Going.*] But—Mr. Fag—tell your master not to be cast down by this.

Fag. Oh, he'll be so disconsolate!

Lucy. And charge him not to think of quarrelling with young Absolute.

Fag. Never fear !—never fear !

Lucy. Be sure—bid him keep up his spirits.

Fag. We will—we will.　　　　　　[*Exeunt severally.*

ACT III

SCENE I.—*The North Parade.*

Enter ABSOLUTE.

Abs. 'Tis just as Fag told me, indeed. Whimsical enough, faith ! My father wants to *force* me to marry the very girl I am plotting to run away with ! He must not know of my connexion with her yet awhile. He has too summary a method of proceeding in these matters. However, I'll read my recantation instantly. My conversion is something sudden, indeed—but I can assure him it is very *sincere.*—So, so, here he comes. He looks plaguy gruff.　　　　　　[*Steps aside.*

Enter SIR ANTHONY.

Sir Anth. No—I'll die sooner than forgive him. *Die*, did I say ? I'll live these fifty years to plague him. At our last meeting, his impudence had almost put me out of temper. An obstinate, passionate, self-willed boy ! Who can he take after ? This is my return for getting him before all his brothers and sisters !—for putting him, at twelve years old, into a marching regiment, and allowing him fifty pounds a year, besides his pay, ever since ! But I have done with him ; he 's anybody's son for me. I never will see him more—never—never—never.

Abs. Now for a penitential face.

Sir Anth. Fellow, get out of my way.

Abs. Sir, you see a penitent before you.

Sir Anth. I see an impudent scoundrel before me.

Abs. A sincere penitent. I am come, sir, to acknowledge my error, and to submit entirely to your will.

Sir Anth. What's that?

Abs. I have been revolving, and reflecting, and considering on your past goodness, and kindness, and condescension to me.

Sir Anth. Well, sir?

Abs. I have been likewise weighing and balancing what you were pleased to mention concerning duty, and obedience, and authority.

Sir Anth. Well, puppy?

Abs. Why then, sir, the result of my reflections is— a resolution to sacrifice every inclination of my own to your satisfaction.

Sir Anth. Why now, you talk sense—absolute sense —I never heard anything more sensible in my life. Confound you! you shall be Jack again.

Abs. I am happy in the appellation.

Sir Anth. Why then, Jack, my dear Jack, I will now inform you who the lady really is. Nothing but your passion and violence, you silly fellow, prevented my telling you at first. Prepare, Jack, for wonder and rapture—prepare. What think you of Miss Lydia Languish?

Abs. Languish! What, the Languishes of Worcestershire.

Sir Anth. Worcestershire! No. Did you never meet Mrs. Malaprop and her niece, Miss Languish, who came into our country just before you were last ordered to your regiment?

Abs. Malaprop! Languish! I don't remember ever to have heard the names before. Yet, stay—I think I do recollect something. *Languish! Languish!* She squints, don't she? A little red-haired girl?

Sir Anth. Squints! A red-haired girl! Z—ds! no.

Abs. Then I must have forgot; it can't be the same person.

Sir Anth. Jack! Jack! what think you of blooming, love-breathing seventeen?

Abs. As to that, sir, I am quite indifferent. If I can please you in the matter, 'tis all I desire.

Sir Anth. Nay, but, Jack, such eyes! such eyes!

so innocently wild ! so bashfully irresolute ! Not a
glance but speaks and kindles some thought of love !
Then, Jack, her cheeks ! her cheeks, Jack ! so deeply
blushing at the insinuations of her tell-tale eyes !
Then, Jack, her lips ! Oh, Jack, lips smiling at their
own discretion ; and if not smiling, more sweetly
pouting ; more lovely in sullenness !

Abs. That 's she indeed. Well done, old gentleman !

Sir Anth. Then, Jack, her neck ! Oh, Jack ! Jack !

Abs. And which is to be mine, sir, the niece or the
aunt ?

Sir Anth. Why, you unfeeling, insensible puppy,
I despise you. When I was of your age, such a description would have made me fly like a rocket ! The
aunt, indeed ! Odds life ! when I ran away with your
mother, I would not have touched anything old or
ugly to gain an empire !

Abs. Not to please your father, sir ?

Sir Anth. To please my father ! Z—ds ! not to
please—— Oh, my father—— Oddso !—yes—yes ;
if my father indeed had desired— That 's quite
another matter. Though he wa'n't the indulgent
father that I am, Jack.

Abs. I dare say not, sir.

Sir Anth. But, Jack, you are not sorry to find your
mistress is so beautiful ?

Abs. Sir, I repeat it ; if I please you in this affair,
'tis all I desire. Not that I think a woman the worse
for being handsome ; but, sir, if you please to recollect,
you before hinted something about a hump or two,
one eye, and a few more graces of that kind. Now,
without being very nice, I own I should rather choose
a wife of mine to have the usual number of limbs and
a limited quantity of back : and though one eye may
be very agreeable, yet as the prejudice has always run
in favour of two, I would not wish to affect a singu-
larity in that article.

Sir Anth. What a phlegmatic sot it is ! Why,
sirrah, you're an anchorite !—a vile insensible stock.

You a soldier! you're a walking block, fit only to dust the company's regimentals on! Odds life! I've a great mind to marry the girl myself!

Abs. I am entirely at your disposal, sir; if you should think of addressing Miss Languish yourself, I suppose you would have me marry the aunt; or if you should change your mind, and take the old lady—'tis the same to me—I'll marry the niece.

Sir Anth. Upon my word, Jack, thou'rt either a very great hypocrite, or—but, come, I know your indifference on such a subject must be all a lie—I'm sure it must—come, now—damn your demure face!—come, confess, Jack—you have been lying—ha'n't you? You have been playing the hypocrite, hey! I'll never forgive you, if you ha'n't been lying and playing the hypocrite.

Abs. I'm sorry, sir, that the respect and duty which I bear to you should be so mistaken.

Sir Anth. Hang your respect and duty! But, come along with me; I'll write a note to Mrs. Malaprop, and you shall visit the lady directly. Her eyes shall be the Promethian torch to you. Come along, I'll never forgive you, if you don't came back stark mad with rapture and impatience—if you don't, egad, I'll marry the girl myself! [*Exeunt.*

SCENE II.—JULIA'S *Dressing-room.*

FAULKLAND *solus.*

Faulk. They told me Julia would return directly; I wonder she is not yet come! How mean does this captious, unsatisfied temper of mine appear to my cooler judgement! Yet I know not that I indulge it in any other point: but on this one subject, and to this one subject, whom I think I love beyond my life, I am ever ungenerously fretful and madly capricious! I am conscious of it—yet I cannot correct myself! What tender honest joy sparkled in her eyes when we met! How delicate was the warmth of her expressions! I was ashamed to appear less happy—

though I had come resolved to wear a face of coolness and upbraiding. Sir Anthony's presence prevented my proposed expostulations : yet I must be satisfied that she has not been so *very* happy in my absence. She is coming ! Yes ! I know the nimbleness of her tread, when she thinks her impatient Faulkland counts the moments of her stay.

Enter JULIA.

Jul. I had not hoped to see you again so soon.

Faulk. Could I, Julia, be contented with my first welcome—restrained as we were by the presence of a third person ?

Jul. O Faulkland, when your kindness can make me thus happy, let me not think that I discovered something of coldness in your first salutation.

Faulk. 'Twas but your fancy, Julia. I *was* rejoiced to see you—to see you in such health. Sure, I had no cause for coldness ?

Jul. Nay, then, I see you have taken something ill. You must not conceal from me what it is.

Faulk. Well, then, shall I own to you that my joy at hearing of your health and arrival here, by your neighbour Acres, was somewhat damped by his dwelling much on the high spirits you had enjoyed in Devonshire—on your mirth—your singing—dancing, and I know not what ? For such is my temper, Julia, that I should regard every mirthful moment in your absence as a treason to constancy : the mutual tear that steals down the cheek of parting lovers is a compact that no smile shall live there till they meet again.

Jul. Must I never cease to tax my Faulkland with this teasing minute caprice ? Can the idle reports of a silly boor weigh in your breast against my tried affection ?

Faulk. They have no weight with me, Julia : no, no —I am happy if you have been so—yet only say, that you did not sing with *mirth*—say that you *thought* of Faulkland in the dance.

Jul. I never can be happy in your absence. If I wear a countenance of content, it is to show that my mind holds no doubt of my Faulkland's truth. If I seemed sad—it were to make malice triumph ; and say, that I had fixed my heart on one, who left me to lament his roving, and my own credulity. Believe me, Faulkland, I mean not to upbraid you when I say, that I have often dressed sorrow in smiles, lest my friends should guess whose unkindness had caused my tears.

Faulk. You were ever all goodness to me. Oh, I am a brute, when I but admit a doubt of your true constancy !

Jul. If ever without such cause from you, as I will not suppose possible, you find my affections veering but a point, may I become a proverbial scoff for levity and base ingratitude.

Faulk. Ah ! Julia, that last word is grating to me. I would I had no title to your *gratitude* ! Search your heart, Julia ; perhaps what you have mistaken for love is but the warm effusion of a too thankful heart !

Jul. For what quality must I love you ?

Faulk. For no quality ! To regard me for any quality of mind or understanding, were only to *esteem* me. And for person—I have often wished myself deformed, to be convinced that I owed no obligation *there* for any part of your affection.

Jul. Where nature has bestowed a show of nice attention in the features of a man, he should laugh at it as misplaced. I have seen men who, in *this* vain article, perhaps, might rank above you; but my heart has never asked my eyes if it were so or not.

Faulk. Now this is not well from *you*, Julia—I despise person in a man—yet, if you loved me as I wish, though I were an Aethiop, you'd think none so fair.

Jul. I see you are determined to be unkind. The *contract* which my poor father bound us in gives you more than a lover's privilege.

Faulk. Again, Julia, you raise ideas that feed and justify my doubts. I would not have been more free —no—I am proud of my restraint. Yet—yet—perhaps your high respect alone for this solemn compact

has fettered your inclinations, which else had made
a worthier choice. How shall I be sure, had you
remained unbound in thought and promise, that I
should still have been the object of your persevering
love ?

Jul. Then try me now. Let us be free as strangers
as to what is past: *my* heart will not feel more liberty !

Faulk. There now ! so hasty, Julia ! so anxious to
be free ! If your love for me were fixed and ardent,
you would not lose your hold, even though I wished it !

Jul. Oh ! you torture me to the heart ! I cannot
bear it.

Faulk. I do not mean to distress you. If I loved
you less, I should never give you an uneasy moment.
But hear me. All my fretful doubts arise from this.
Women are not used to weigh, and separate the motives
of their affections : the cold dictates of prudence,
gratitude, or filial duty, may sometimes be mistaken
for the pleadings of the heart. I would not boast—
yet let me say, that I have neither age, person, nor
character to found dislike on ; my fortune, such as
few ladies could be charged with indiscretion in the
match. O Julia ! when *Love* receives such countenance from *Prudence*, nice minds will be suspicious
of its birth.

Jul. I know not whither your insinuations would
tend : but as they seem pressing to insult me, I will
spare you the regret of having done so. I have given
you no cause for this !　　　　　　　　[*Exit in tears.*

Faulk. In tears ! stay, Julia : stay but for a moment.
The door is fastened !—Julia ! my soul—but for one
moment !—I hear her sobbing ! 'Sdeath ! what a brute
am I to use her thus ! Yet stay. Aye, she is coming
now : how little resolution there is in woman ! how
a few soft words can turn them ! No, faith ! she is
not coming either. Why, Julia—my love—say but
that you forgive me—come but to tell me that. Now
this is being *too* resentful : stay ! she is coming too
—I thought she would—no steadiness in anything !
her going away must have been a mere trick then--

she shan't see that I was hurt by it. I'll affect indifference. [*Hums a tune ; then listens.*] No: Z—ds!
she's *not* coming !—nor don't intend it, I suppose.
This is not steadiness, but obstinacy ! Yet I deserve
it. What, after so long an absence to quarrel with her
tenderness !—'twas barbarous and unmanly ! I should
be ashamed to see her now. I'll wait till her just
resentment is abated—and when I distress her so
again, may I lose her for ever ! and be linked instead
to some antique virago, whose gnawing passions, and
long hoarded spleen, shall make me curse my folly half
the day and all the night. [*Exit.*

SCENE III.—MRS. MALAPROP'S *Lodgings.*

MRS. MALAPROP, *with a letter in her hand, and* CAPTAIN
ABSOLUTE.

Mrs. Mal. Your being Sir Anthony's son, captain,
would itself be a sufficient accommodation ; but from
the ingenuity of your appearance, I am convinced you
deserve the character here given of you.

Abs. Permit me to say, madam, that as I never
yet have had the pleasure of seeing Miss Languish, my
principal inducement in this affair at present is the
honour of being allied to Mrs. Malaprop ; of whose
intellectual accomplishments, elegant manners, and un-
affected learning, no tongue is silent.

Mrs. Mal. Sir, you do me infinite honour ! I beg,
captain, you'll be seated. [*Sit.*] Ah ! few gentlemen,
nowadays, know how to value the ineffectual qualities
in a woman ! few think how a little knowledge becomes
a gentlewoman ! Men have no sense now but for the
worthless flower of beauty !

Abs. It is but too true indeed, ma'am ; yet I fear
our ladies should share the blame—they think our
admiration of beauty so great, that knowledge in them
would be superfluous. Thus, like garden trees, they
seldom show fruit, till time has robbed them of the
more specious blossom. Few, like Mrs. Malaprop and
the orange-tree, are rich in both at once !

Mrs. Mal. Sir, you overpower me with good-breeding. He is the very pineapple of politeness !—You are not ignorant, captain, that this giddy girl has somehow contrived to fix her affections on a beggarly, strolling, eaves-dropping ensign, whom none of us have seen, and nobody knows anything of ?

Abs. Oh, I have heard the silly affair before. I'm not at all prejudiced against her on *that* account.

Mrs. Mal. You are very good and very considerate, captain. I am sure I have done everything in my power since I exploded the affair ; long ago I laid my positive conjunctions on her, never to think on the fellow again ; I have since laid Sir Anthony's preposition before her ; but, I am sorry to say, she seems resolved to decline every particle that I enjoin her.

Abs. It must be very distressing, indeed, ma'am.

Mrs. Mal. Oh ! it gives me the hydrostatics to such a degree. I thought she had persisted from corresponding with him ; but, behold, this very day I have interceded another letter from the fellow ; I believe I have it in my pocket.

Abs. Oh, the devil ! my last note.   [*Aside.*

Mrs. Mal. Aye, here it is.

Abs. Aye, my note indeed ! Oh, the little traitress Lucy.   [*Aside.*

Mrs. Mal. There, perhaps you may know the writing.   [*Gives him the letter.*

Abs. I think I have seen the hand before—yes, I certainly must have seen this hand before——

Mrs. Mal. Nay, but read it, captain.

Abs. [Reads.] '*My soul's idol, my adored Lydia !* ' Very tender indeed !

Mrs. Mal. Tender ! aye, and profane too, o' my conscience !

Abs. ' *I am excessively alarmed at the intelligence you send me, the more so as my new rival——* '

Mrs. Mal. That 's *you*, sir.

Abs. ' *Has universally the character of being an accomplished gentleman, and a man of honour——* ' Well, that 's handsome enough.

Mrs. Mal. Oh, the fellow has some design in writing so.

Abs. That he had, I'll answer for him, ma'am.

Mrs. Mal. But go on, sir—you'll see presently.

Abs. ' *As for the old weather-beaten she-dragon who guards you* '—who can he mean by that ?

Mrs. Mal. Me, sir ! *me*—he means *me* ! There—what do you think now ?—but go on a little further.

Abs. Impudent scoundrel !—' *it shall go hard but I will elude her vigilance, as I am told that the same ridiculous vanity, which makes her dress up her coarse features, and deck her dull chat with hard words which she don't understand*——'

Mrs. Mal. There, sir, an attack upon my language ! what do you think of that ?—an aspersion upon my parts of speech ! was ever such a brute ! Sure, if I reprehend anything in this world, it is the use of my oracular tongue, and a nice derangement of epitaphs !

Abs. He deserves to be hanged and quartered ! let me see—' *same ridiculous vanity*——'

Mrs. Mal. You need not read it again, sir.

Abs. I beg pardon, ma'am—' *does also lay her open to the grossest deceptions from flattery and pretended admiration* '—an impudent coxcomb !—' *so that I have a scheme to see you shortly with the old harridan's consent, and even to make her a go-between in our interview.*'—Was ever such assurance !

Mrs. Mal. Did you ever hear anything like it ?—he'll elude my vigilance, will he ?—yes, yes ! ha ! ha ! he's very likely to enter these doors !—we'll try who can plot best !

Abs. So we will, ma'am—so we will. Ha! ha! ha! a conceited puppy, ha ! ha ! ha ! Well, but, Mrs. Malaprop, as the girl seems so infatuated by this fellow, suppose you were to wink at her corresponding with him for a little time—let her even plot an elopement with him—then do you connive at her escape—while *I*, just in the nick, will have the fellow laid by the heels, and fairly contrive to carry her off in his stead.

Mrs. Mal. I am delighted with the scheme; never was anything better perpetrated !

Abs. But, pray, could not I see the lady for a few minutes now ?—I should like to try her temper a little.

Mrs. Mal. Why, I don't know. I doubt she is not prepared for a visit of this kind. There is a decorum in these matters.

Abs. O Lord ! she won't mind *me*—only tell her Beverley——

Mrs. Mal. Sir !

Abs. Gently, good tongue.   [*Aside.*

Mrs. Mal. What did you say of Beverley ?

Abs. Oh, I was going to propose that you should tell her, by way of jest, that it was Beverley who was below—she'd come down fast enough then—ha ! ha ! ha !

Mrs. Mal. 'Twould be a trick she well deserves— besides, you know the fellow tells her he'll get my consent to see her—ha ! ha ! Let him if he can, I say again. Lydia, come down here ! [*Calling.*] He'll make me a *go-between in their interviews !*—ha ! ha ! ha ! Come down, I say, Lydia ! I don't wonder at your laughing, ha ! ha ! ha ! his impudence is truly ridiculous.

Abs. 'Tis very ridiculous, upon my soul, ma'am, ha ! ha ! ha !

Mrs. Mal. The little hussy won't hear. Well, I'll go and tell her at once who it is—she shall know that Captain Absolute is come to wait on her. And I'll make her behave as becomes a young woman.

Abs. As you please, ma'am.

Mrs. Mal. For the present, captain, your servant. Ah ! you've not done laughing yet, I see—*elude my vigilance !* yes, yes ; ha ! ha ! ha !   [*Exit.*

Abs. Ha ! ha ! ha ! one would think now that I might throw off all disguise at once, and seize my prize with security ; but such is Lydia's caprice, that to undeceive were probably to lose her. I'll see whether she knows me.

> [*Walks aside, and seems engaged in looking at the pictures.*

E

Enter LYDIA.

Lyd. What a scene am I now to go through ! surely nothing can be more dreadful than to be obliged to listen to the loathsome addresses of a stranger to one's heart. I have heard of girls persecuted as I am, who have appealed in behalf of their favoured lover to the generosity of his rival : suppose I were to try it—there stands the hated rival—an officer too !—but oh, how unlike my Beverley ! I wonder he don't begin—truly he seems a very negligent wooer !—quite at his ease, upon my word !—I'll speak first—Mr. Absolute.

Abs. Ma'am.   [*Turns round.*

Lyd. O heavens ! Beverley !

Abs. Hush !—hush, my life ! softly ! be not surprised !

Lyd. I am so astonished ! and so terrified ! and so overjoyed !—for Heaven's sake ! how came you here ?

Abs. Briefly—I have deceived your aunt. I was informed that my new rival was to visit here this evening, and contriving to have him kept away, have passed myself on *her* for Captain Absolute.

Lyd. Oh, charming ! And she really takes you for young Absolute ?

Abs. Oh, she's convinced of it.

Lyd. Ha ! ha ! ha ! I can't forbear laughing to think how her sagacity is over-reached !

Abs. But we trifle with our precious moments—such another opportunity may not occur—then let me now conjure my kind, my condescending angel, to fix the time when I may rescue her from undeserving persecution, and with a licensed warmth plead for my reward.

Lyd. Will you then, Beverley, consent to forfeit that portion of my paltry wealth ?—that burden on the wings of love ?

Abs. Oh, come to me—rich only thus—in loveliness. Bring no portion to me but thy love—'twill be generous in you, Lydia—for well you know, it is the only dower your poor Beverley can repay.

Lyd. How persuasive are his words !—how charming will poverty be with him !

Abs. Ah ! my soul, what a life will we then live ? Love shall be our idol and support ! we will worship him with a monastic strictness ; abjuring all worldly toys, to centre every thought and action there. Proud of calamity, we will enjoy the wreck of wealth ; while the surrounding gloom of adversity shall make the flame of our pure love show doubly bright. By heavens ! I would fling all goods of fortune from me with a prodigal hand, to enjoy the scene where I might clasp my Lydia to my bosom, and say, the world affords no smile to me—but here. [*Embracing her.*] If she holds out now, the devil is in it !   [*Aside.*

Lyd. Now could I fly with him to the Antipodes ! but my persecution is not yet come to a crisis.

Enter MRS. MALAPROP, *listening.*

Mrs. Mal. I am impatient to know how the little hussy deports herself.   [*Aside.*

Abs. So pensive, Lydia !—is then your warmth abated?

Mrs. Mal. Warmth abated !—so !—she has been in a passion, I suppose.

Lyd. No—nor ever can while I have life.

Mrs. Mal. An ill-tempered little devil ! She'll be in a passion all her life—will she ?

Lyd. Think not the idle threats of my ridiculous aunt can ever have any weight with me.

Mrs. Mal. Very dutiful, upon my word !

Lyd. Let her choice be Captain Absolute, but Beverley is mine.

Mrs. Mal. I am astonished at her assurance !—to his face—this is to his face !

Abs. Thus then let me enforce my suit.   [*Kneeling.*

Mrs. Mal. Aye, poor young man !—down on his knees entreating for pity ! I can contain no longer. —Why, thou vixen ! I have overheard you.

Abs. Oh, confound her vigilance !   [*Aside.*

Mrs. Mal. Captain Absolute—I know not how to apologize for her shocking rudeness.

Abs. So all 's safe, I find. [*Aside.*]—I have hopes, madam, that time will bring the young lady——

Mrs. Mal. Oh, there 's nothing to be hoped for from her ! she 's as headstrong as an allegory on the banks of Nile.

Lyd. Nay, madam, what do you charge me with now ?

Mrs. Mal. Why, thou unblushing rebel—didn't you tell this gentleman to his face that you loved another better ?—didn't you say you never would be his ?

Lyd. No, madam—I did not.

Mrs. Mal. Good heavens ! what assurance ! Lydia, Lydia, you ought to know that lying don't become a young woman ! Didn't you boast that Beverley— that stroller Beverley, possessed your heart ? Tell me that, I say.

Lyd. 'Tis true, ma'am, and none but *Beverley*——

Mrs. Mal. Hold !—hold, Assurance !—you shall not be so rude.

Abs. Nay, pray, Mrs. Malaprop, don't stop the young lady's speech : she 's very welcome to talk thus —it does not hurt *me* in the least, I assure you.

Mrs. Mal. You are *too* good, captain—*too* amiably patient—but come with me, miss.—Let us see you again soon, captain—remember what we have fixed.

Abs. I shall, ma'am.

Mrs. Mal. Come, take a graceful leave of the gentleman.

Lyd. May every blessing wait on my *Beverley*, my loved *Bev*——

Mrs. Mal. Hussy ! I'll choke the word in your throat —come along—come along.   [*Exeunt severally.*

[BEVERLEY *kissing his hand to* LYDIA—MRS.
MALAPROP *stopping her from speaking.*

SCENE IV.—ACRES'S *Lodgings.*

ACRES *and* DAVID.

ACRES *as just dressed.*

Acres. Indeed, David—do you think I become it so ?

Dav. You are quite another creature, believe me,

master. By the mass! an' we've any luck we shall
see the Devon monkerony in all the print-shops in
Bath!

Acres. Dress *does* make a difference, David.

Dav. 'Tis all in all, I think—difference! why, an'
you were to go now to Clod Hall I am certain the old
lady wouldn't know you : Master Butler wouldn't
believe his own eyes, and Mrs. Pickle would cry,
' Lard presarve me! ' our dairymaid would come gig-
gling to the door, and I warrant Dolly Tester, your
honour's favourite, would blush like my waistcoat.
Oons! I'll hold a gallon, there an't a dog in the house
but would bark, and I question whether Phillis would
wag a hair of her tail!

Acres. Aye, David, there's nothing like polishing.

Dav. So I says of your honour's boots ; but the boy
never heeds me!

Acres. But, David, has Mr. De-la-grace been here?
I must rub up my balancing, and chasing, and boring.

Dav. I'll call again, sir.

Acres. Do—and see if there are any letters for me at
the post-office.

Dav. I will. By the mass, I can't help looking at
your head !—if I hadn't been by at the cooking, I wish
I may die if I should have known the dish again myself !   [*Exit.*

ACRES *comes forward, practising a dancing step.*

Acres. Sink, slide, coupee. Confound the first in-
ventors of cotillons! say I—they are as bad as algebra
to us country gentlemen. I can walk a minuet easy
enough when I am forced !—and I have been accounted
a good stick in a country-dance. Odds jigs and
tabours !—I never valued your cross-over to couple—
figure in—right and left—and I'd foot it with e'er
a captain in the county !—but these outlandish heathen
allemandes and cotillons are quite beyond me! I shall
never prosper at 'em, that's sure—mine are true-born
English legs—they don't understand their curst French
lingo !—their *pas* this, and *pas* that, and *pas* t'other!

—damn me ! my feet don't like to be called Paws !
No, 'tis certain I have most Antigallican toes !

Enter SERVANT.

Serv. Here is Sir Lucius O'Trigger to wait on you
sir.

Acres. Show him in.

Enter SIR LUCIUS.

Sir Luc. Mr. Acres, I am delighted to embrace you.

Acres. My dear Sir Lucius, I kiss your hands.

Sir Luc. Pray, my friend, what has brought you so
suddenly to Bath ?

Acres. Faith ! I have followed Cupid's Jack-a-
lantern, and find myself in a quagmire at last. In
short, I have been very ill-used, Sir Lucius. I don't
choose to mention names, but look on me as on a very
ill-used gentleman.

Sir Luc. Pray, what is the case ? I ask no names.

Acres. Mark me, Sir Lucius, I fall as deep as need
be in love with a young lady—her friends take my part
—I follow her to Bath—send word of my arrival ; and
receive answer, that the lady is to be otherwise disposed of. This, Sir Lucius, I call being ill-used.

Sir Luc. Very ill, upon my conscience. Pray, can
you divine the cause of it ?

Acres. Why, there's the matter : she has another
lover, one Beverley, who, I am told, is now in Bath.
Odds slanders and lies ! he must be at the bottom
of it.

Sir Luc. A rival in the case, is there ?—and you
think he has supplanted you unfairly ?

Acres. Unfairly ! to be sure he has. He never could
have done it fairly.

Sir Luc. Then sure you know what is to be done !

Acres. Not I, upon my soul !

Sir Luc. We wear no swords here, but you understand me.

Acres. What ! fight him !

Sir Luc. Aye, to be sure : what can I mean else ?

Acres. But he has given me no provocation.

Sir Luc. Now, I think he has given you the greatest provocation in the world. Can a man commit a more heinous offence against another than to fall in love with the same woman? Oh, by my soul! it is the most unpardonable breach of friendship.

Acres. Breach of friendship! Aye, aye; but I have no acquaintance with this man. I never saw him in my life.

Sir Luc. That's no argument at all—he has the less right, then, to take such a liberty.

Acres. Gad, that's true—I grow full of anger, Sir Lucius! I fire apace! Odds hilts and blades! I find a man may have a deal of valour in him, and not know it! But couldn't I contrive to have a little right of my side?

Sir Luc. What the devil signifies *right*, when your *honour* is concerned? Do you think Achilles or my little Alexander the Great ever inquired where the right lay? No, by my soul, they drew their broadswords, and left the lazy sons of peace to settle the justice of it.

Acres. Your words are a grenadier's march to my heart! I believe courage must be catching! I certainly do feel a kind of valour rising as it were—a kind of courage, as I may say. Odds flints, pans, and triggers! I'll challenge him directly.

Sir Luc. Ah, my little friend! if I had Blunderbuss Hall here—I could show you a range of ancestry, in the O'Trigger line, that would furnish the new room; every one of whom had killed his man! For though the mansion-house and dirty acres have slipped through my fingers, I thank Heaven our honour and the family pictures are as fresh as ever.

Acres. Oh, Sir Lucius! I have had ancestors too! —every man of 'em colonel or captain in the militia! Odds balls and barrels! say no more—I'm braced for it. The thunder of your words has soured the milk of human kindness in my breast! Z—ds! as the man in the play says, 'I could do such deeds—— '

Sir Luc. Come, come, there must be no passion at all in the case—these things should always be done civilly.

Acres. I must be in a passion, Sir Lucius—I must be in a rage. Dear Sir Lucius, let me be in a rage, if you love me. Come, here 's pen and paper. [*Sits down to write.*] I would the ink were red! Indite, I say, indite! How shall I begin? Odds bullets and blades! I'll write a good bold hand, however.

Sir Luc. Pray compose yourself.

Acres. Come—now, shall I begin with an oath? Do, Sir Lucius, let me begin with a damme.

Sir Luc. Pho! pho! do the thing decently, and like a Christian. Begin now—' *Sir*——'

Acres. That 's too civil by half.

Sir Luc. ' *To prevent the confusion that might arise*——'

Acres. Well——

Sir Luc. ' *from our both addressing the same lady*——'

Acres. Aye—there 's the reason—' *same lady* '— well——

Sir Luc. ' *I shall expect the honour of your company*——'

Acres. Z—ds! I'm not asking him to dinner.

Sir Luc. Pray, be easy.

Acres. Well then, ' *honour of your company*——'

Sir Luc. ' *to settle our pretensions*——'

Acres. Well.

Sir Luc. Let me see—aye, King's Mead Fields will do—' *in King's Mead Fields.*'

Acres. So that 's done. Well, I'll fold it up presently; my own crest—a hand and dagger—shall be the seal.

Sir Luc. You see now this little explanation will put a stop at once to all confusion or misunderstanding that might arise between you.

Acres. Aye, we fight to prevent any misunderstanding.

Sir Luc. Now, I'll leave you to fix your own time. Take my advice, and you'll decide it this evening if you can; then let the worst come of it, 'twill be off your mind to-morrow.

Acres. Very true.

Sir Luc. So I shall see nothing more of you, unless it be by letter, till the evening. I would do myself the honour to carry your message ; but, to tell you a secret, I believe I shall have just such another affair on my own hands. There is a gay captain here, who put a jest on me lately, at the expense of my country, and I only want to fall in with the gentleman, to call him out.

Acres. By my valour, I should like to see you fight first ! Odds life ! I should like to see you kill him, if it was only to get a little lesson.

Sir Luc. I shall be very proud of instructing you. Well, for the present—but remember now, when you meet your antagonist, do everything in a mild and agreeable manner. Let your courage be as keen, but at the same time as polished, as your sword.

                      [Exeunt severally.

ACT IV

Scene I.—Acres's *Lodgings.*

Acres *and* David.

Dav. Then, by the mass, sir ! I would do no such thing—ne'er a Sir Lucius O'Trigger in the kingdom should make me fight, when I wa'n't so minded. Oons! what will the old lady say, when she hears o't ?

Acres. Ah ! David, if you had heard Sir Lucius ! Odds sparks and flames ! he would have roused your valour.

Dav. Not he, indeed. I hates such bloodthirsty cormorants. Look'ee, master, if you'd wanted a bout at boxing, quarter-staff, or short-staff, I should never be the man to bid you cry off : but for your cursed sharps and snaps, I never knew any good come of 'em.

Acres. But my honour, David, my honour ! I must be very careful of my honour.

Dav. Aye, by the mass ! and I would be very careful

of it ; and I think in return my honour couldn't do
less than to be very careful of me.

Acres. Odds blades ! David, no gentleman will ever
risk the loss of his honour !

Dav. I say, then, it would be but civil in honour
never to risk the loss of a gentleman. Look'ee, master,
this honour seems to me to be a marvellous false
friend : aye, truly, a very courtier-like servant. Put
the case, I was a gentleman (which, thank God, no
one can say of me) ; well—my honour makes me
quarrel with another gentleman of my acquaintance.
So—we fight. (Pleasant enough that.) Boh !—I kill
him—(the more 's my luck). Now, pray who gets the
profit of it ? Why, my honour. But put the case
that he kills me !—by the mass ! I go to the worms,
and my honour whips over to my enemy.

Acres. No, David—in that case !—odds crowns and
laurels ! your honour follows you to the grave.

Dav. Now, that 's just the place where I could make
a shift to do without it.

Acres. Z—ds ! David, you are a coward ! It doesn't
become my valour to listen to you. What, shall I disgrace my ancestors ? Think of that, David—think
what it would be to disgrace my ancestors !

Dav. Under favour, the surest way of not disgracing
them, is to keep as long as you can out of their company. Look'ee now, master, to go to them in such
haste—with an ounce of lead in your brains—I should
think might as well be let alone. Our ancestors are
very good kind of folks ; but they are the last people
I should choose to have a visiting acquaintance with.

Acres. But, David, now, you don't think there is
such very, very, *very* great danger, hey ? Odds life !
people often fight without any mischief done !

Dav. By the mass, I think 'tis ten to one against
you ! Oons ! here to meet some lion-headed fellow,
I warrant, with his d—n'd double-barrelled swords,
and cut-and-thrust pistols ! Lord bless us ! it makes
me tremble to think o't ! Those be such desperate
bloody-minded weapons ! Well, I never could abide

'em—from a child I never could fancy 'em : I suppose there a'n't been so merciless a beast in the world as your loaded pistol !

Acres. Z—ds ! I *won't* be afraid. Odds fire and fury ! you shan't make me afraid. Here is the challenge, and I have sent for my dear friend Jack Absolute to carry it for me.

Dav. Aye, i' the name of mischief, let *him* be the messenger. For my part, I wouldn't lend a hand to it for the best horse in your stable. By the mass ! it don't look like another letter ! It is, as I may say, a designing and malicious-looking letter ; and I warrant smells of gunpowder like a soldier's pouch ! Oons ! I wouldn't swear it mayn't go off !

Acres. Out, you poltroon !—you ha'n't the valour of a grasshopper.

Dav. Well, I say no more—'twill be sad news, to be sure, at Clod Hall !—but I ha' done. How Phillis will howl when she hears of it !—Aye, poor bitch, she little thinks what shooting her master's going after !—And I warrant old Crop, who has carried your honour, field and road, these ten years, will curse the hour he was born. [*Whimpering.*

Acres. It won't do, David—I am determined to fight —so get along, you coward—while I'm in the mind.

Enter SERVANT.

Serv. Captain Absolute, sir.

Acres. Oh ! show him up. [*Exit* SERVANT.

Dav. Well, Heaven send we be all alive this time to-morrow.

Acres. What 's that !—Don't provoke me, David !

Dav. Good-bye, master. [*Whimpering.*

Acres. Get along, you cowardly, dastardly, croaking raven. [*Exit* DAVID.

Enter ABSOLUTE.

Abs. What 's the matter, Bob?

Acres. A vile, sheep-hearted blockhead !—If I hadn't the valour of St. George and the dragon to boot——

Abs. But what did you want with me, Bob ?

Acres. Oh !—There——   [*Gives him the challenge.*

Abs. '*To Ensign Beverley.*' So—what's going on now ! [*Aside.*]—Well, what's this ?

Acres. A challenge !

Abs. Indeed !—Why, you won't fight him ; will you, Bob ?

Acres. 'Egad, but I will, Jack. Sir Lucius has wrought me to it. He has left me full of rage—and I'll fight this evening, that so much good passion mayn't be wasted.

Abs. But what have I to do with this ?

Acres. Why, as I think you know something of this fellow, I want you to find him out for me, and give him this mortal defiance.

Abs. Well, give it to me, and trust me he gets it.

Acres. Thank you, my dear friend, my dear Jack ; but it is giving you a great deal of trouble.

Abs. Not in the least—I beg you won't mention it. No trouble in the world, I assure you.

Acres. You are very kind. What it is to have a friend ! You couldn't be my second—could you, Jack ?

Abs. Why, no, Bob—not in *this* affair—it would not be quite so proper.

Acres. Well, then, I must get my friend Sir Lucius. I shall have your good wishes, however, Jack.

Abs. Whenever he meets you, believe me.

Enter SERVANT.

Serv. Sir Anthony Absolute is below, inquiring for the captain.

Abs. I'll come instantly.—Well, my little hero, success attend you.   [*Going.*

Acres. Stay—stay, Jack. If Beverley should ask you what kind of a man your friend Acres is, do tell him I am a devil of a fellow—will you, Jack ?

Abs. To be sure I shall. I'll say you are a determined dog—hey, Bob !

Acres. Aye, do, do—and if that frightens him, egad,

perhaps he mayn't come. So tell him I generally kill
a man a-week ; will you, Jack ?

Abs. I will, I will ; I'll say you are called in the
country ' Fighting Bob.'

Acres. Right—right—'tis all to prevent mischief ;
for I don't want to take his life if I clear my honour.

Abs. No ! that 's very kind of you.

Acres. Why, you don't wish me to kill him—do you,
Jack ?

Abs. No, upon my soul, I do not. But a devil of a
fellow, hey ?   [*Going.*

Acres. True, true—but stay—stay, Jack—you may
add, that you never saw me in such a rage before—a
most devouring rage !

Abs. I will, I will.

Acres. Remember, Jack—a determined dog !

Abs. Aye, aye, ' Fighting Bob.'   [*Exeunt severally.*

SCENE II.—Mrs. Malaprop's *Lodgings.*

Mrs. Malaprop *and* Lydia.

Mrs. Mal. Why, thou perverse one !—tell me what
you can object to him ? Isn't he a handsome man ?—
tell me that. A genteel man ? a pretty figure of a man ?

Lyd. She little thinks whom she is praising ! [*Aside.*]
—So is Beverley, ma'am.

Mrs. Mal. No caparisons, miss, if you please. Caparisons don't become a young woman.—No ! Captain
Absolute is indeed a fine gentleman !

Lyd. Aye, the Captain Absolute *you* have seen.
                                                    [*Aside.*

Mrs. Mal. Then he 's *so* well bred ; *so* full of alacrity,
and adulation ! and has *so much* to say for himself :
in such good language too ! His physiognomy so
grammatical ! Then his presence is so noble ! I protest when I saw him, I thought of what Hamlet says in
the play :—' Hesperian curls—the front of Job himself !
—an eye, like March, to threaten at command !—a
station, like Harry Mercury, new—' Something about

kissing—on a hill—however, the similitude struck me directly.

Lyd. How enraged she'll be presently when she discovers her mistake !   [*Aside.*

Enter SERVANT.

Serv. Sir Anthony and Captain Absolute are below, ma'am.

Mrs. Mal. Show them up here.   [*Exit* SERVANT. Now, Lydia, I insist on your behaving as becomes a young woman. Show your good breeding, at least, though you have forgot your duty.

Lyd. Madam, I have told you my resolution ! I shall not only give him no encouragement, but I won't even speak to, or look at him.

[*Flings herself into a chair, with her face from the door.*

Enter SIR ANTHONY *and* ABSOLUTE.

Sir Anth. Here we are, Mrs. Malaprop ; come to mitigate the frowns of unrelenting beauty,—and difficulty enough I had to bring this fellow. I don't know what's the matter ; but if I had not held him by force, he'd have given me the slip.

Mrs. Mal. You have infinite trouble, Sir Anthony, in the affair. I am ashamed for the cause !—Lydia, Lydia, rise, I beseech you !—pay your respects !
                    [*Aside to her.*

Sir Anth. I hope, madam, that Miss Languish has reflected on the worth of this gentleman, and the regard due to her aunt's choice, and *my* alliance.—Now, Jack ! speak to her.   [*Aside to him.*

Abs. What the devil shall I do ! [*Aside.*]—You see, sir, she won't even look at me, whilst you are here. I knew she wouldn't !—I told you so. Let me entreat you, sir, to leave us together !

                    [ABSOLUTE *seems to expostulate with his father.*

Lyd. [*Aside.*] I wonder I ha'n't heard my aunt exclaim yet ! sure she can't have looked at him !— perhaps their regimentals are alike, and she is something blind.

Sir Anth. I say, sir, I won't stir a foot yet.

Mrs. Mal. I am sorry to say, Sir Anthony, that my affluence over my niece is very small.—Turn round, Lydia, I blush for you !   [*Aside to her.*

Sir Anth. May I not flatter myself, that Miss Languish will assign what cause of dislike she can have to my son ! —Why don't you begin, Jack ?—Speak, you puppy— speak !   [*Aside to him.*

Mrs. Mal. It is impossible, Sir Anthony, she can have any.—She will not say she has.—Answer, hussy ! why don't you answer ?   [*Aside to her.*

Sir Anth. Then, madam, I trust that a childish and hasty predilection will be no bar to Jack's happiness.— Z—ds ! sirrah ! why don't you speak !   [*Aside to him.*

Lyd. [*Aside.*] I think my lover seems as little in- clined to conversation as myself.—How strangely blind my aunt must be !

Abs. Hem ! hem ! Madam—hem ! [ABSOLUTE *at- tempts to speak, then returns to* SIR ANTHONY.] Faith, sir, I am so confounded !—and—so—so—confused ! I told you I should be so, sir,—I knew it. The—the —tremor of my passion entirely takes away my presence of mind.

Sir Anth. But it don't take away your voice, fool, does it? Go up, and speak to her directly !

          [ABSOLUTE *makes signs to* MRS. MALAPROP *to leave them together.*

Mrs. Mal. Sir Anthony, shall we leave them together ?—Ah ! you stubborn little vixen !

                              [*Aside to her.*

Sir Anth. Not yet, ma'am, not yet !—What the devil are you at ? unlock your jaws, sirrah, or—

          [*Aside to him.* ABSOLUTE *draws near* LYDIA.

Abs. Now Heaven send she may be too sullen to look round !—I must disguise my voice.   [*Aside.* [*Speaks in a low hoarse tone.*]—Will not Miss Languish lend an ear to the mild accents of true love ? Will not—

Sir Anth. What the devil ails the fellow ? Why don't you speak out ?—not stand croaking like a frog in a quinsy !

Abs. The—the—excess of my awe, and my—my—my modesty, quite choke me !

Sir Anth. Ah ! your *modesty* again !—I'll tell you what, Jack ; if you don't speak out directly, and glibly too, I shall be in such a rage !—Mrs. Malaprop, I wish the lady would favour us with something more than a side-front.   [MRS. MALAPROP *seems to chide* LYDIA.

Abs. So all will out I see !—[*Goes up to* LYDIA, *speaks softly*]. Be not surprised, my Lydia, suppress all surprise at present.

Lyd. [*Aside.*] Heavens, 'tis Beverley's voice ! Sure he can't have imposed on Sir Anthony too !

[*Looks round by degrees, then starts up.*
Is this possible ! my Beverley !—how can this be ?—my Beverley ?

Abs. Ah ! 'tis all over.   [*Aside.*

Sir Anth. Beverley !—the devil—Beverley !—What can the girl mean ?—This is my son, Jack Absolute.

Mrs. Mal. For shame, hussy ! for shame !—your head runs so on that fellow, that you have him always in your eyes !—beg Captain Absolute's pardon directly.

Lyd. I see no Captain Absolute, but my loved Beverley !

Sir Anth. Z—ds ! the girl's mad !—her brain's turned by reading !

Mrs. Mal. O' my conscience, I believe so !—What do you mean by Beverley, hussy? You saw Captain Absolute before to-day ; there he is—your husband that shall be.

Lyd. With all my soul, ma'am—when I refuse my Beverley——

Sir Anth. Oh ! she's as mad as Bedlam !—or has this fellow been playing us a rogue's trick !—Come here, sirrah, who the devil are you ?

Abs. Faith, sir, I am not quite clear myself ; but I'll endeavour to recollect.

Sir Anth. Are you my son or not ?—answer for your mother, you dog, if you won't for me.

Mrs. Mal. Aye, sir, who are you ? O mercy ! I begin to suspect !

Abs. Ye powers of impudence, befriend me ! [*Aside.*]
Sir Anthony, most assuredly I am your wife's son ; and
that I sincerely believe myself to be *yours* also, I hope
my duty has always shown.—Mrs. Malaprop, I am your
most respectful admirer, and shall be proud to add
affectionate nephew.—I need not tell my Lydia, that
she sees her faithful *Beverley*, who, knowing the singular
generosity of her temper, assumed that name, and a
station, which has proved a test of the most disin-
terested love, which he now hopes to enjoy in a more
elevated character.

Lyd. So !—there will be no elopement after all !
[*Sullenly.*

Sir Anth. Upon my soul, Jack, thou art a very impudent fellow ! To do you justice, I think I never saw a
piece of more consummate assurance !

Abs. Oh, you flatter me, sir—you compliment—'tis
my *modesty*, you know, sir—my *modesty* that has stood
in my way.

Sir Anth. Well, I am glad you are not the dull, insensible varlet you pretended to be, however !—I'm glad
you have made a fool of your father, you dog—I am.
So this was your *penitence*, your *duty*, and *obedience* !
I thought it was d—n'd sudden !—You *never heard their
names before*, not you ! *What, the Languishes of
Worcestershire,* hey ?—*if you could please me in the
affair, 'twas all you desired !* Ah ! you dissembling
villain !—What ! [*pointing to* LYDIA] *she squints, don't
she ?—a little red-haired girl !*—hey ? Why, you hypo-
critical young rascal—I wonder you a'n't ashamed to
hold up your head !

Abs. 'Tis with difficulty, sir—I *am* confused—very
much confused, as you must perceive.

Mrs. Mal. O Lud ! Sir Anthony !—a new light
breaks in upon me !—hey !—how ! what ! captain, did
you write the letters then ? What—am I to thank
you for the elegant compilation of ' *an old weather-
beaten she-dragon* '—hey ? O mercy !—was it *you*
that reflected on my parts of speech ?

Abs. Dear sir ! my modesty will be overpowered at

F

last, if you don't assist me. I shall certainly not be
able to stand it !

Sir Anth. Come, come, Mrs. Malaprop, we must forget
and forgive. Odds life! matters have taken so clever a
turn all of a sudden that I could find in my heart to be
so good-humoured! and so gallant! hey! Mrs. Malaprop!

Mrs. Mal. Well, Sir Anthony, since *you* desire it,
we will not anticipate the past ; so mind, young people,
our retrospection will be all to the future.

Sir Anth. Come, we must leave them together ;
Mrs. Malaprop, they long to fly into each other's arms,
I warrant !—Jack—isn't the cheek as I said, hey ?—
and the eye, you rogue !—and the lip—hey ? Come,
Mrs. Malaprop, we'll not disturb their tenderness—
theirs is the time of life for happiness !—' *Youth 's
the season made for joy*' [*sings*]—hey! Odds life ! I'm
in such spirits—I don't know what I could not do !
Permit me, ma'am. [*Gives his hand to* MRS. MALA-
PROP. *Sings.*] Tol-de-rol—'gad, I should like to have
a little fooling myself—Tol-de-rol ! de-rol !

> [*Exit singing and handing* MRS. MALAPROP.
> LYDIA *sits sullenly in her chair.*

Abs. So much thought bodes me no good. [*Aside.*]
—So grave, Lydia !

Lyd. Sir !

Abs. So !—egad ! I thought as much !—that d—n'd
monosyllable has froze me ! [*Aside.*]—What, Lydia,
now that we are as happy in our friends' consent, as in
our mutual vows——

Lyd. Friends' consent, indeed !   [*Peevishly.*

Abs. Come, come, we must lay aside some of our
romance—a little *wealth* and *comfort* may be endured
after all. And for your fortune, the lawyers shall make
such settlements as——

Lyd. Lawyers ! I hate lawyers !

Abs. Nay, then, we will not wait for their lingering
forms, but instantly procure the licence, and——

Lyd. The *licence* !—I hate licence !

Abs. Oh, my love ! be not so unkind !—thus let me
entreat——   [*Kneeling.*

Lyd. Pshaw!—what signifies kneeling, when **you** know I *must* have you?

Abs. [*Rising.*] Nay, madam, there shall be no constraint upon your inclinations, I promise you.   If I have lost your heart—I resign the rest.—'Gad, I must try what a little spirit will do.   [*Aside.*

Lyd. [*Rising.*] Then, sir, let me tell you, the interest you had there was acquired by a mean, unmanly imposition, and deserves the punishment of fraud. What, you have been treating *me* like a child!—humouring my romance! and laughing, I suppose, at your success!

Abs. You wrong me, Lydia, you wrong me—only hear——

Lyd. So, while *I* fondly imagined we were deceiving my relations, and flattered myself that I should outwit and incense them all—behold my hopes are to be crushed at once, by my aunt's consent and approbation—and *I* am myself the only dupe at last!   [*Walking about in a heat.*]   But here, sir, here is the picture— Beverley's picture! [*taking a miniature from her bosom*] which I have worn, night and day, in spite of threats and entreaties!   There, sir [*flings it to him*], and be assured I throw the original from my heart as easily.

Abs. Nay, nay, ma'am, we will not differ as to that. Here [*taking out a picture*], here is Miss Lydia Languish. What a difference!—aye, *there* is the heavenly assenting smile that first gave soul and spirit to my hopes! —those are the lips which sealed a vow, as yet scarce dry in Cupid's calendar!—and there the half-resentful blush, that *would* have checked the ardour of my thanks.   Well, all that's past!—all over indeed! There, madam—in beauty, that copy is not equal to you, but in mind its merit over the original, in being still the same, is such—that—I cannot find in my heart to part with it.   [*Puts it up again.*

Lyd. [*Softening.*] 'Tis *your own* doing, sir—I, I, I suppose you are perfectly satisfied.

Abs. Oh, most certainly—sure, now, this is **much better than** being in love!—ha! ha! ha!—there's

some spirit in *this*! What signifies breaking some
scores of solemn promises : all that's of no consequence,
you know. To be sure people will say, that miss didn't
know her own mind—but never mind that !—or, perhaps, they may be ill-natured enough to hint that the
gentleman grew tired of the lady and forsook her—
but don't let that fret you.

Lyd. There's no bearing his insolence.
                                          [*Bursts into tears.*

Enter MRS. MALAPROP *and* SIR ANTHONY.

Mrs. Mal. [*Entering.*] Come, we must interrupt your
billing and cooing awhile.

Lyd. This is worse than your treachery and deceit,
you base ingrate.   [*Sobbing.*

Sir Anth. What the devil's the matter now ! Z—ds !
Mrs. Malaprop, this is the oddest billing and cooing
I ever heard !—but what the deuce is the meaning
of it ? I am quite astonished !

Abs. Ask the lady, sir.

Mrs. Mal. Oh, mercy ! I'm quite analysed, for my
part !—why, Lydia, what is the reason of this ?

Lyd. Ask the gentleman, ma'am.

Sir Anth. Z—ds ! I shall be in a frenzy !—why,
Jack, you are not come out to be any one else, are
you ?

Mrs. Mal. Aye, sir, there's no more trick, is there ?
—you are not like Cerberus, three gentlemen at once,
are you ?

Abs. You'll not let me speak—I say the lady can
account for this much better than I can.

Lyd. Ma'am, you once commanded me never to
think of Beverley again—there is the man—I now
obey you : for, from this moment, I renounce him for
ever.   [*Exit* LYDIA.

Mrs. Mal. Oh, mercy ! and miracles ! what a turn
here is--why sure, captain, you haven't behaved dis-
respectfully to my niece ?

Sir Anth. Ha ! ha ! ha !—ha ! ha ! ha !—now I see

it. Ha! ha! ha!—now I see it—you have been too
lively, Jack.

Abs. Nay, sir, upon my word——

Sir Anth. Come, no lying, Jack—I'm sure 'twas so.

Mrs. Mal. O Lud! Sir Anthony! Oh, fie, captain!

Abs. Upon my soul, ma'am——

Sir Anth. Come, no excuses, Jack; why, your father,
you rogue, was so before you : the blood of the Abso-
lutes was always impatient. Ha! ha! ha! poor little
Lydia!—why, you've frightened her, you dog, you
have.

Abs. By all that's good, sir——

Sir Anth. Z—ds! say no more, I tell you—Mrs.
Malaprop shall make your peace. You must make
his peace, Mrs. Malaprop : you must tell her 'tis
Jack's way—tell her 'tis all our ways—it runs in the
blood of our family! Come away, Jack. Ha! ha!
ha! Mrs. Malaprop—a young villain!

　　　　　　　　　　　　　　　　[Pushes him out.

Mrs. Mal. Oh! Sir Anthony! Oh, fie, captain!

　　　　　　　　　　　　　　　　[Exeunt severally.

SCENE III.—*The North Parade.*

Enter SIR LUCIUS O'TRIGGER.

Sir Luc. I wonder where this Captain Absolute hides
himself. Upon my conscience!—these officers are
always in one's way in love affairs : I remember
I might have married Lady Dorothy Carmine, if it
had not been for a little rogue of a major, who ran
away with her before she could get a sight of me!
And I wonder too what it is the ladies can see in them
to be so fond of them—unless it be a touch of the old
serpent in 'em, that makes the little creatures be caught,
like vipers, with a bit of red cloth. Ha! isn't this
the captain coming?—faith it is! There is a prob-
ability of succeeding about that devil, that is mighty
provoking! Who the devil is he talking to?

　　　　　　　　　　　　　　　　[Steps aside.

Enter CAPTAIN ABSOLUTE.

Abs. To what fine purpose I have been plotting! a noble reward for all my schemes, upon my soul!— a little gipsy!—I did not think her romance could have made her so d—n'd absurd either. 'Sdeath, I never was in a worse humour in my life! I could cut my own throat, or any other person's, with the greatest pleasure in the world!

Sir Luc. Oh, faith! I'm in the luck of it. I never could have found him in a sweeter temper for my purpose—to be sure I'm just come in the nick! now to enter into conversation with him, and so quarrel genteelly. [SIR LUCIUS *goes up to* ABSOLUTE.] With regard to that matter, captain, I must beg leave to differ in opinion with you.

Abs. Upon my word, then, you must be a very subtle disputant: because, sir, I happened just then to be giving no opinion at all.

Sir Luc. That's no reason. For give me leave to tell you, a man may *think* an untruth as well as speak one.

Abs. Very true, sir, but if a man never utters his thoughts, I should think they might stand a chance of escaping controversy.

Sir Luc. Then, sir, you differ in opinion with me, which amounts to the same thing.

Abs. Hark'ee, Sir Lucius—if I had not before known you to be a gentleman, upon my soul I should not have discovered it at this interview: for what you can drive at, unless you mean to quarrel with me, I cannot conceive!

Sir Luc. I humbly thank you, sir, for the quickness of your apprehension [*bowing*]—you have named the very thing I would be at.

Abs. Very well, sir—I shall certainly not baulk your inclinations: but I should be glad you would please to explain your motives.

Sir Luc. Pray, sir, be easy—the quarrel is a very pretty quarrel as it stands—we should only spoil it by trying to explain it. However, your memory is

very short, or you could not have forgot an affront
you passed on me within this week. So, no more, but
name your time and place.

Abs. Well, sir, since you are so bent on it, the sooner
the better ; let it be this evening—here by the Spring
Gardens. We shall scarcely be interrupted.

Sir Luc. Faith ! that same interruption in affairs of
this nature shows very great ill-breeding.   I don't
know what 's the reason, but in England, if a thing of
this kind gets wind, people make such a pother,
that a gentleman can never fight in peace and
quietness.   However, if it 's the same to you, captain,
I should take it as a particular kindness if you'd let
us meet in King's Mead Fields, as a little business will
call me there about six o'clock, and I may dispatch
both matters at once.

Abs. 'Tis the same to me exactly. A little after six,
then, we will discuss this matter more seriously.

Sir Luc. If you please, sir ; there will be very pretty
small-sword light, though it won't do for a long shot.
So that matter 's settled ! and my mind 's at ease.

[*Exit* SIR LUCIUS.

Enter FAULKLAND, *meeting* ABSOLUTE.

Abs. Well met. I was going to look for you. O
Faulkland ! all the demons of spite and disappointment have conspired against me ! I'm so vexed, that
if I had not the prospect of a resource in being knocked
o' the head by and by, I should scarce have spirits to
tell you the cause.

Faulk. What can you mean ? Has Lydia changed
her mind ? I should have thought her duty and inclination would now have pointed to the same object.

Abs. Aye, just as the eyes do of a person who squints :
when her love eye was fixed on me, t'other—her eye
of duty—was finely obliqued : but when duty bid her
point that the same way, off t'other turned on a
swivel, and secured its retreat with a frown !

Faulk. But what 's the resource you——

Abs. Oh, to wind up the whole, a good-natured

Irishman here has [*mimicking* SIR LUCIUS] begged leave
to have the pleasure of cutting my throat—and I mean
to indulge him—that 's all.

Faulk.   Prithee, be serious.

Abs.   'Tis fact, upon my soul.   Sir Lucius O'Trigger
—you know him by sight—for some affront, which
I am sure I never intended, has obliged me to meet
him this evening at six o'clock : 'tis on that account
I wished to see you—you must go with me.

Faulk.   Nay, there must be some mistake, sure.   Sir
Lucius shall explain himself—and I dare say matters
may be accommodated : but this evening, did you
say ?—I wish it had been any other time.

Abs.   Why ?—there will be light enough : there will
(as Sir Lucius says) ' be very pretty small-sword light,
though it will not do for a long shot.'   Confound his
long shots !

Faulk.   But I am myself a good deal ruffled, by a
difference I have had with Julia—my vile tormenting
temper has made me treat her so cruelly, that I shall
not be myself till we are reconciled.

Abs.   By heavens! Faulkland, you don't deserve her.

Enter SERVANT, *gives* FAULKLAND *a letter.*

Faulk.   O Jack ! this is from Julia—I dread to
open it ! I fear it may be to take a last leave—perhaps
to bid me return her letters—and restore——Oh ! how
I suffer for my folly !

Abs.   Here—let me see.   [*Takes the letter and opens it.*]
Aye, a final sentence, indeed !—'tis all over with you,
faith !

Faulk.   Nay, Jack—don't keep me in suspense.

Abs.   Hear, then.   ' *As I am convinced that my dear
Faulkland's own reflections have already upbraided him
for his last unkindness to me, I will not add a word on
the subject.   I wish to speak with you as soon as possible.
Yours ever and truly,* JULIA.'—There 's stubbornness
and resentment for you.   [*Gives him the letter.*]   Why,
man, you don't seem one whit the happier at this.

Faulk.   Oh, yes, I am—but—but——

Abs. Confound your *buts.* You never hear anything that would make another man bless himself, but you immediately d—n it with a *but.*

Faulk. Now, Jack, as you are my friend, own honestly— don't you think there is something forward—something indelicate in this haste to forgive ? Women should never sue for reconciliation : that should always come from *us.* They should retain their coldness till *woo'd* to kindness—and their *pardon,* like their *love,* should ' not unsought be won.'

Abs. I have not patience to listen to you : thou'rt incorrigible !—so say no more on the subject. I must go to settle a few matters—let me see you before six— remember—at my lodgings. A poor industrious devil like me, who have toiled, and drudged, and plotted to gain my ends, and am at last disappointed by other people's folly, may in pity be allowed to swear and grumble a little ; but a captious sceptic in love, a slave to fretfulness and whim—who has no difficulties but of his own creating—is a subject more fit for ridicule than compassion !   [*Exit* ABSOLUTE.

Faulk. I feel his reproaches : yet I would not change this too exquisite nicety for the gross content with which *he* tramples on the thorns of love. His engaging me in this duel has started an idea in my head, which I will instantly pursue. I'll use it as the touchstone of Julia's sincerity and disinterestedness : if her love prove pure and sterling ore, my name will rest on it with honour !—and once I've stamped it there, I lay aside my doubts for ever : but if the dross of selfish- ness, the allay of pride predominate—'twill be best to leave her as a toy for some less cautious fool to sigh for.   [*Exit* FAULKLAND.

ACT V

Scene I.—Julia's *Dressing-room.*

Julia *sola.*

Jul. How this message has alarmed me! what dreadful accident can he mean? why such charge to be alone? O Faulkland!—how many unhappy moments!—how many tears have you cost me!

Enter Faulkland.

Jul. What means this?—why this caution, Faulkland?

Faulk. Alas! Julia, I am come to take a long farewell.

Jul. Heavens! what do you mean?

Faulk. You see before you a wretch, whose life is forfeited. Nay, start not!—the infirmity of my temper has drawn all this misery on me. I left you fretful and passionate—an untoward accident drew me into a quarrel—the event is, that I must fly this kingdom instantly. O Julia, had I been so fortunate as to have called you mine entirely, before this mischance had fallen on me, I should not so deeply dread my banishment!

Jul. My soul is oppressed with sorrow at the nature of your misfortune: had these adverse circumstances arisen from a less fatal cause I should have felt strong comfort in the thought that I could now chase from your bosom every doubt of the warm sincerity of my love. My heart has long known no other guardian—I now entrust my person to your honour—we will fly together. When safe from pursuit, my father's will may be fulfilled—and I receive a legal claim to be the partner of your sorrows, and tenderest comforter. Then on the bosom of your wedded Julia you may lull your keen regret to slumbering; while virtuous love, with a cherub's hand, shall smooth the brow of upbraiding thought, and pluck the thorn from compunction.

Faulk. O Julia! I am bankrupt in gratitude! but the time is so pressing, it calls on you for so hasty a resolution. Would you not wish some hours to

weigh the advantages you forgo, and what little
compensation poor Faulkland can make you beside
his solitary love ?

Jul. I ask not a moment. No, Faulkland, I have
loved you for yourself : and if I now, more than ever,
prize the solemn engagement which so long has pledged
us to each other, it is because it leaves no room for
hard aspersions on my fame, and puts the seal of duty
to an act of love. But let us not linger. Perhaps this
delay——

Faulk. 'Twill be better I should not venture out again
till dark. Yet am I grieved to think what numberless
distresses will press heavy on your gentle disposition !

Jul. Perhaps your fortune may be forfeited by this
unhappy act. I know not whether 'tis so—but sure
that alone can never make us unhappy. The little
I have will be sufficient to support us ; and exile never
should be splendid.

Faulk. Aye, but in such an abject state of life my
wounded pride perhaps may increase the natural fretfulness of my temper, till I become a rude, morose
companion, beyond your patience to endure. Perhaps
the recollection of a deed my conscience cannot justify
may haunt me in such gloomy and unsocial fits, that
I shall hate the tenderness that would relieve me,
break from your arms, and quarrel with your fondness !

Jul. If your thoughts should assume so unhappy
a bent you will the more want some mild and affectionate spirit to watch over and console you: one who,
by bearing *your* infirmities with gentleness and resig-
nation, may teach you *so* to bear the evils of your
fortune.

Faulk. Julia, I have proved you to the quick ! and
with this useless device I throw away all my doubts.
How shall I plead to be forgiven this last unworthy
effect of my restless, unsatisfied disposition ?

Jul. Has no such disaster happened as you related ?

Faulk. I am ashamed to own that it was pretended ; yet in pity, Julia, do not kill me with resent-
ing a fault which never can be repeated : but sealing,

this once, my pardon, let me to-morrow, in the face
of Heaven, receive my future guide and monitress, and
expiate my past folly by years of tender adoration.

Jul. Hold, Faulkland!—that you are free from
a crime, which I before feared to name, Heaven knows
how sincerely I rejoice! These are tears of thankful-
ness for that! But that your cruel doubts should have
urged you to an imposition that has wrung my heart,
gives me now a pang more keen than I can express!

Faulk. By heavens! Julia——

Jul. Yet hear me. My father loved you, Faulkland! and you preserved the life that tender parent
gave me; in his presence I pledged my hand—joyfully
pledged it—where before I had given my heart. When,
soon after, I lost that parent, it seemed to me that
Providence had, in Faulkland, shown me whither to
transfer, without a pause, my grateful duty, as well as
my affection: hence I have been content to bear from
you what pride and delicacy would have forbid me from
another. I will not upbraid you by repeating how
you have trifled with my sincerity.

Faulk. I confess it all! yet hear——

Jul. After such a year of trial, I might have flattered
myself that I should not have been insulted with a new
probation of my sincerity, as cruel as unnecessary!
I now see it is not in your nature to be content, or
confident in love. With this conviction—I never will
be yours. While I had hopes that my persevering
attention, and unreproaching kindness, might in time
reform your temper, I should have been happy to have
gained a dearer influence over you; but I will not
furnish you with a licensed power to keep alive an
incorrigible fault, at the expense of one who never
would contend with you.

Faulk. Nay, but, Julia, by my soul and honour, if
after this——

Jul. But one word more. As my faith has once
been given to you, I never will barter it with another.
I shall pray for your happiness with the truest sincerity;
and the dearest blessing I can ask of Heaven to send

you, will be to charm you from that unhappy temper, which alone has prevented the performance of our solemn engagement. All I request of *you* is, that you will yourself reflect upon this infirmity, and when you number up the many true delights it has deprived you of, let it not be your *least* regret, that it lost you the love of one who would have followed you in beggary through the world ! [*Exit.*

Faulk. She 's gone !—for ever ! There was an awful resolution in her manner, that riveted me to my place. O fool !—dolt !—barbarian !—cursed as I am with more imperfections than my fellow wretches, kind Fortune sent a heaven-gifted cherub to my aid, and, like a ruffian, I have driven her from my side ! I must now haste to my appointment. Well, my mind is tuned for such a scene. I shall wish only to become a principal in it, and reverse the tale my cursed folly put me upon forging here. O Love !—tormentor !— fiend !—whose influence, like the moon's, acting on men of dull souls, makes idiots of them, but meeting subtler spirits, betrays their course, and urges sensibility to madness ! [*Exit.*

Enter MAID *and* LYDIA.

Maid. My mistress, ma'am, I know, was here just now—perhaps she is only in the next room. [*Exit* MAID.

Lyd. Heigh ho ! Though he has used me so, this fellow runs strangely in my head I believe one lecture from my grave cousin will make me recall him.

Enter JULIA

Lyd. O Julia, I am come to you with such an appetite for consolation. Lud ! child, what 's the matter with you ? You have been crying ! I'll be hanged, if that Faulkland has not been tormenting you !

Jul. You mistake the cause of my uneasiness ! Something *has* flurried me a little. Nothing that you can guess at.—I would not accuse Faulkland to a sister ! [*Aside.*

Lyd. Ah! whatever vexations you may have, I can assure you mine surpass them. You know who Beverley proves to be?

Jul. I will now own to you, Lydia, that Mr. Faulkland had before informed me of the whole affair. Had young Absolute been the person you took him for I should not have accepted your confidence on the subject, without a serious endeavour to counteract your caprice.

Lyd. So, then, I see I have been deceived by every one!—but I don't care—I'll never have him.

Jul. Nay, Lydia——

Lyd. Why, is it not provoking? when I thought we were coming to the prettiest distress imaginable, to find myself made a mere Smithfield bargain of at last. There had I projected one of the most sentimental elopements!—so becoming a disguise!—so amiable a ladder of ropes! Conscious moon—four horses—Scotch parson—with such surprise to Mrs. Malaprop —and such paragraphs in the newspapers! Oh, I shall die with disappointment!

Jul. I don't wonder at it!

Lyd. Now—sad reverse!—what have I to expect, but, after a deal of flimsy preparation, with a bishop's licence, and my aunt's blessing, to go simpering up to the altar; or perhaps be cried three times in a country church, and have an unmannerly fat clerk ask the consent of every butcher in the parish to join John Absolute and Lydia Languish, spinster! Oh, that I should live to hear myself called spinster!

Jul. Melancholy, indeed!

Lyd. How mortifying, to remember the dear delicious shifts I used to be put to, to gain half a minute's conversation with this fellow! How often have I stole forth, in the coldest night in January, and found him in the garden, stuck like a dripping statue! There would he kneel to me in the snow, and sneeze and cough so pathetically! he shivering with cold and I with apprehension! and while the freezing blast numbed our joints, how warmly would he press me to pity his flame, and glow with mutual ardour ! Ah, Julia, that was something like being in love.

Jul. If I were in spirits, Lydia, I should chide you only by laughing heartily at you ; but it suits more the situation of my mind, at present, earnestly to entreat you, not to let a man, who loves you with sincerity, suffer that unhappiness from your caprice, which I know too well caprice can inflict.

Lyd. O Lud ! what has brought my aunt here ?

Enter MRS. MALAPROP, FAG, *and* DAVID.

Mrs. Mal. So ! so ! here 's fine work !—here 's fine suicide, paracide, and simulation going on in the fields ! and Sir Anthony not to be found to prevent the antistrophe !

Jul. For Heaven's sake, madam, what 's the meaning of this ?

Mrs. Mal. That gentleman can tell you—'twas he enveloped the affair to me.

Lyd. Do, sir, will you, inform us ?   [*To* FAG.

Fag. Ma'am, I should hold myself very deficient in every requisite that forms the man of breeding, if I delayed a moment to give all the information in my power to a lady so deeply interested in the affair as you are.

Lyd. But quick ! quick, sir !

Fag. True, ma'am, as you say, one should be quick in divulging matters of this nature ; for should we be tedious, perhaps while we are flourishing on the subject two or three lives may be lost !

Lyd. O patience ! Do, ma'am, for Heaven's sake, tell us what is the matter ?

Mrs. Mal. Why ! murder 's the matter ! slaughter 's the matter ! killing 's the matter !—but he can tell you the perpendiculars.

Lyd. Then, prithee, sir, be brief.

Fag. Why, then, ma'am, as to murder, I cannot take upon me to say—and as to slaughter, or manslaughter, that will be as the jury finds it.

Lyd. But who, sir—who are engaged in this ?

Fag. Faith, ma'am, one is a young gentleman whom

I should be very sorry anything was to happen to—
a very pretty behaved gentleman ! We have lived
much together, and always on terms.

Lyd. But who is this ? who ! who ! who !

Fag. My master, ma'am—my master—I speak of my
master.

Lyd. Heavens ! What, Captain Absolute !

Mrs. Mal. Oh, to be sure, you are frightened now !

Jul. But who are with him, sir ?

Fag. As to the rest, ma'am, this gentleman can inform you better than I.

Jul. Do speak, friend.   [*To* DAVID.

Dav. Look'ee, my lady—by the mass ! there 's mischief going on. Folks don't use to meet for amusement with firearms, firelocks, fire-engines, fire-screens,
fire-office, and the devil knows what other crackers
beside ! This, my lady, I say, has an angry savour.

Jul. But who is there beside Captain Absolute,
friend ?

Dav. My poor master—under favour for mentioning
him first. You know me, my lady—I am David—
and my master of course is, or *was*, Squire Acres.
Then comes Squire Faulkland.

Jul. Do, ma'am, let us instantly endeavour to
prevent mischief.

Mrs. Mal. Oh, fie—it would be very inelegant in
us : we should only participate things.

Dav. Ah ! do, Mrs. Aunt, save a few lives—they
are desperately given, believe me. Above all, there is
that bloodthirsty Philistine, Sir Lucius O'Trigger.

Mrs. Mal. Sir Lucius O'Trigger ! Oh, mercy ! have
they drawn poor little dear Sir Lucius into the scrape?
Why, how you stand, girl ! you have no more feeling
than one of the Derbyshire petrefactions !

Lyd. What are we to do, madam ?

Mrs. Mal. Why, fly with the utmost felicity, to be
sure, to prevent mischief !—here, friend—you can show
us the place ?

Fag. If you please, ma'am, I will conduct you.—
David, do you look for Sir Anthony.   [*Exit* DAVID

Mrs. Mal. Come, girls !—this gentleman will exhort us. Come, sir, you're our envoy—lead the way, and we'll precede.

Fag. Not a step before the ladies for the world !

Mrs. Mal. You're sure you know the spot ?

Fag. I think I can find it, ma'am ; and one good thing is, we shall hear the report of the pistols as we draw near, so we can't well miss them ; never fear, ma'am, never fear.　　　　　　　　*[Exit, he talking.*

Scene II.—*South Parade.*

Enter Absolute, *putting his sword under his great-coat.*

Abs. A sword seen in the streets of Bath would raise as great an alarm as a mad dog. How provoking this is in Faulkland !—never punctual ! I shall be obliged to go without him at last. Oh, the devil ! here 's Sir Anthony !—how shall I escape him ?

　　　　[Muffles up his face, and takes a circle to go off.

Enter Sir Anthony.

Sir Anth. How one may be deceived at a little distance ! only that I see he don't know me, I could have sworn that was Jack ! Hey !—Gad's life ! it is. Why, Jack—what are you afraid of ? hey !—sure I'm right. Why, Jack—Jack Absolute !　　　　　*[Goes up to him.*

Abs. Really, sir, you have the advantage of me : I don't remember ever to have had the honour—my name is Saunderson, at your service.

Sir Anth. Sir, I beg your pardon—I took you—hey ? —why, z—ds ! it is—Stay——　　*[Looks up to his face.]* So, so—your humble servant, Mr. Saunderson ! Why, you scoundrel, what tricks are you after now ?

Abs. Oh ! a joke, sir, a joke ! I came here on purpose to look for you, sir.

Sir Anth. You did ! well, I am glad you were so lucky : but what are you muffled up so for ?—what 's this for ?—hey ?

Abs. 'Tis cool, sir ; isn't it ?—rather chilly somehow : but I shall be late—I have a particular engagement.

Sir Anth. Stay. Why, I thought you were looking for me ? Pray, Jack, where is't you are going ?

Abs. Going, sir !

Sir Anth. Aye—where are you going ?

Abs. Where am I going ?

Sir Anth. You unmannerly puppy !

Abs. I was going, sir, to—to—to—to Lydia—sir, to Lydia—to make matters up if I could ; and I was looking for you, sir, to—to——

Sir Anth. To go with you, I suppose. Well, come along.

Abs. Oh ! z—ds ! no, sir, not for the world ! I wished to meet with you, sir—to—to—to—You find it cool, I'm sure, sir—you'd better not stay out.

Sir Anth. Cool !—not at all. Well, Jack—and what will you say to Lydia ?

Abs. Oh, sir, beg her pardon, humour her—promise and vow : but I detain you, sir—consider the cold air on your gout.

Sir Anth. Oh, not at all !—not at all !—I'm in no hurry. Ah ! Jack, you youngsters when once you are wounded here. [*Putting his hand to* ABSOLUTE'S *breast.*] Hey ! what the deuce have you got here ?

Abs. Nothing, sir—nothing.

Sir Anth. What 's this ?—here 's something d—n'd hard.

Abs. Oh, trinkets, sir ! trinkets—a bauble for Lydia !

Sir Anth. Nay, let me see your taste. [*Pulls his coat open, the sword falls.*] Trinkets !—a bauble for Lydia ! z—ds ! sirrah, you are not going to cut her throat, are you ?

Abs. Ha ! ha ! ha !—I thought it would divert you, sir, though I didn't mean to tell you till afterwards.

Sir Anth. You didn't ? Yes, this is a very diverting trinket, truly.

Abs. Sir, I'll explain to you. You know, sir, Lydia is romantic—dev'lish romantic, and very absurd of course : now, sir, I intend, if she refuses to forgive me —to unsheathe this sword—and swear—I'll fall upon its point, and expire at her feet !

Sir Anth. Fall upon a fiddlestick's end !—why, I suppose it is the very thing that would please her. Get along, you fool !

Abs. Well, sir, you shall hear of my success—you shall hear—' O Lydia !—forgive me, or this pointed steel '—says I.

Sir Anth. ' O booby ! stab away, and welcome '—says she. Get along !—and d—n your trinkets !

[*Exit* ABSOLUTE.

Enter DAVID, *running.*

Dav. Stop him ! stop him ! Murder ! thief ! fire !—Stop fire ! stop fire !—Oh, Sir Anthony—call ! call ! bid 'm stop ! Murder ! fire !

Sir Anth. Fire ! murder ! where ?

Dav. Oons ! he 's out of sight ! and I'm out of breath, for my part ! Oh, Sir Anthony, why didn't you stop him ? why didn't you stop him ?

Sir Anth. Z—ds ! the fellow 's mad ! Stop whom ? stop Jack ?

Dav. Aye, the captain, sir !—there 's murder and slaughter——

Sir Anth. Murder !

Dav. Aye, please you, Sir Anthony, there 's all kinds of murder, all sorts of slaughter to be seen in the fields : there 's fighting going on, sir—bloody sword-and-gun fighting !

Sir Anth. Who are going to fight, dunce ?

Dav. Everybody that I know of, Sir Anthony : everybody is going to fight, my poor master, Sir Lucius O'Trigger, your son, the captain——

Sir Anth. Oh, the dog !—I see his tricks ; do you know the place ?

Dav. King's Mead Fields.

Sir Anth. You know the way ?

Dav. Not an inch ; but I'll call the mayor—aldermen — constables — churchwardens — and beadles — we can't be too many to part them.

Sir Anth. Come along — give me your shoulder ! we'll get assistance as we go—the lying villain ! Well,

I shall be in such a frenzy. So—this was the history
of his trinkets ! I'll bauble him !   [*Exeunt.*

SCENE III.—*King's Mead Fields.*

SIR LUCIUS *and* ACRES, *with pistols.*

Acres. By my valour ! then, Sir Lucius, forty yards
is a good distance. Odds levels and aims !—I say it is
a good distance.

Sir Luc. Is it for muskets or small field-pieces ?
Upon my conscience, Mr. Acres, you must leave those
things to me. Stay now—I'll show you. [*Measures
paces along the stage.*]   There now, that is a very pretty
distance—a pretty gentleman's distance.

Acres. Z—ds ! we might as well fight in a sentry-
box ! I tell you, Sir Lucius, the farther he is off, the
cooler I shall take my aim.

Sir Luc. Faith ! then I suppose you would aim at
him best of all if he was out of sight !

Acres. No, Sir Lucius, but I should think forty or
eight-and-thirty yards——

Sir Luc. Pho ! pho ! nonsense ! three or four feet
between the mouths of your pistols is as good as a mile.

Acres. Odds bullets, no !—by my valour ! there is
no merit in killing him so near : no, my dear Sir Lucius,
let me bring him down at a long shot : a long shot,
Sir Lucius, if you love me !

Sir Luc. Well—the gentleman's friend and I must
settle that. But tell me now, Mr. Acres, in case of
an accident, is there any little will or commission I
could execute for you !

Acres. I am much obliged to you, Sir Lucius—but
I don't understand——

Sir Luc. Why, you may think there's no being shot
at without a little risk, and if an unlucky bullet
should carry a quietus with it—I say it will be no time
then to be bothering you about family matters.

Acres. A quietus !

Sir Luc. For instance, now—if that should be the

case—would you choose to be pickled and sent home?
—or would it be the same to you to lie here in the
Abbey? I'm told there is very snug lying in the
Abbey.

Acres. Pickled!—snug lying in the Abbey! Odds
tremors! Sir Lucius, don't talk so!

Sir Luc. I suppose, Mr. Acres, you never were
engaged in an affair of this kind before?

Acres. No, Sir Lucius, never before.

Sir Luc. Ah! that's a pity!—there's nothing like
being used to a thing. Pray now, how would you
receive the gentleman's shot?

Acres. Odds files!—I've practised that—there, Sir
Lucius—there. [*Puts himself in an attitude.*] A side-
front, hey? Odds! I'll make myself small enough:
I'll stand edgeways.

Sir Luc. Now—you're quite out—for if you stand
so when I take my aim——   [*Levelling at him.*

Acres. Z—ds! Sir Lucius—are you sure it is not
cocked?

Sir Luc. Never fear.

Acres. But—but—you don't know—it may go off
of its own head!

Sir Luc. Pho! be easy. Well, now if I hit you in
the body, my bullet has a double chance—for if it
misses a vital part of your right side, 'twill be very
hard if it don't succeed on the left!

Acres. A vital part!

Sir Luc. But, there—fix yourself so [*placing him*]—let
him see the broad-side of your full front—there—now
a ball or two may pass clean through your body, and
never do any harm at all.

Acres. Clean through me!—a ball or two clean
through me!

Sir Luc. Aye—may they—and it is much the
genteelest attitude into the bargain.

Acres. Look'ee! Sir Lucius—I'd just as lieve be
shot in an awkward posture as a genteel one—so, by
my valour! I will stand edgeways.

Sir Luc. [*Looking at his watch.*] Sure they don't

mean to disappoint us. Hah !—no, faith—I think I
see them coming.

Acres. Hey !—what !—coming !——

Sir Luc. Aye—who are those yonder getting over
the stile ?

Acres. There are two of them, indeed !—well—let
them come—hey, Sir Lucius !—we—we—we—we—
won't run.

Sir Luc. Run !

Acres. No—I say—we *won't* run, by my valour !

Sir Luc. What the devil's the matter with you ?

Acres. Nothing—nothing—my dear friend—my dear
Sir Lucius—but I—I—I don't feel quite so bold, somehow, as I did.

Sir Luc. Oh, fie !—consider your honour.

Acres. Aye—true—my honour. Do, Sir Lucius,
edge in a word or two every now and then about my
honour.

Sir Luc. Well, here they're coming.   [*Looking*

Acres. Sir Lucius—if I wa'n't with you, I should
almost think I was afraid—if my valour should leave
me ! Valour will come and go.

Sir Luc. Then pray keep it fast, while you have it.

Acres. Sir Lucius—I doubt it is going—yes—my
valour is certainly going !—it is sneaking off ! I feel
it oozing out as it were at the palms of my hands !

Sir Luc. Your honour—your honour. Here they
are.

Acres. Oh, mercy !—now—that I was safe at Clod
Hall ! or could be shot before I was aware !

Enter FAULKLAND *and* ABSOLUTE.

Sir Luc. Gentlemen, your most obedient. Hah !—
what, Captain Absolute ! So, I suppose, sir, you are
come here, just like myself—to do a kind office, first
for your friend—then to proceed to business on your
own account.

Acres. What, Jack !—my dear Jack !—my dear
friend !

Abs. Heark 'ee, Bob, *Beverley* 's at hand.

Sir Luc. Well, Mr. Acres—I don't blame your salut-ing the gentleman civilly.—So, Mr. Beverley [*to* FAULK-LAND] if you'll choose your weapons, the captain and I will measure the ground.

Faulk. My weapons, sir ?

Acres. Odds life ! Sir Lucius, I'm not going to fight Mr. Faulkland ; these are my particular friends.

Sir Luc. What, sir, did not you come here to fight Mr. Acres ?

Faulk. Not I, upon my word, sir.

Sir Luc. Well, now, that's mighty provoking ! But I hope, Mr. Faulkland, as there are three of us come on purpose for the game—you won't be so cantankerous as to spoil the party by sitting out.

Abs. Oh, pray, Faulkland, fight to oblige Sir Lucius.

Faulk. Nay, if Mr. Acres is so bent on the matter——

Acres. No, no, Mr. Faulkland—I'll bear my dis-appointment like a Christian. Look'ee, Sir Lucius, there's no occasion at all for me to fight ; and if it is the same to you, I'd as lieve let it alone.

Sir Luc. Observe me, Mr. Acres—I must not be trifled with. You have certainly challenged some-body—and you came here to fight him. Now, if that gentleman is willing to represent him—I can't see, for my soul, why it isn't just the same thing.

Acres. Why, no—Sir Lucius—I tell you, 'tis one Beverley I've challenged—a fellow, you see, that dare not show his face ! If *he* were here, I'd make him give up his pretensions directly !

Abs. Hold, Bob—let me set you right—there is no such man as Beverley in the case. The person who assumed that name is before you ; and as his preten-sions are the same in both characters, he is ready to support them in whatever way you please.

Sir Luc Well, this is lucky. Now you have an opportunity——

Acres. What, quarrel with my dear friend Jack Absolute—not if he were fifty Beverleys ! Z—ds ! Sir Lucius, you would not have me so unnatural.

Sir Luc. Upon my conscience, Mr. Acres, your valour has *oozed* away with a vengeance!

Acres. Not in the least! Odds backs and abettors! I'll be your second with all my heart—and if you should get a *quietus*, you may command me entirely. I'll get you *snug lying* in the *Abbey here*; or *pickle* you, and send you over to Blunderbuss Hall, or anything of the kind, with the greatest pleasure.

Sir Luc. Pho! pho! you are little better than a coward.

Acres. Mind, gentlemen, he calls me a *coward*; coward was the word, by my valour!

Sir Luc. Well, sir?

Acres. Look'ee, Sir Lucius, 'tisn't that I mind the word coward—*coward* may be said in joke—but if you had call'd me a *poltroon*, odds daggers and balls——

Sir Luc. Well, sir?

Acres. I should have thought you a very ill-bred man.

Sir Luc. Pho! you are beneath my notice.

Abs. Nay, Sir Lucius, you can't have a better second than my friend Acres. He is a most *determined dog*— called in the country, *Fighting Bob*. He generally *kills a man a week*; don't you, Bob?

Acres. Aye—at home!

Sir Luc. Well, then, captain, 'tis we must begin—so come out, my little counsellor [*draws his sword*], and ask the gentleman, whether he will resign the lady, without forcing you to proceed against him?

Abs. Come on then, sir [*draws*]; since you won't let it be an amicable suit, here's my reply.

Enter Sir Anthony, David, *and the* Women.

Dav. Knock 'em all down, sweet Sir Anthony, knock down my master in particular—and bind his hands over to their good behaviour!

Sir Anth. Put up, Jack, put up, or I shall be in a frenzy—how came you in a duel, sir?

Abs. Faith, sir, that gentleman can tell you better than I; 'twas he called on me, and you know, sir, I serve his majesty.

Sir Anth. Here's a pretty fellow! I catch him going to cut a man's throat, and he tells me, he serves his majesty! Zounds! sirrah, then how durst you draw the king's sword against one of his subjects?

Abs. Sir, I tell you! that gentleman called me out, without explaining his reasons.

Sir Anth. Gad! sir, how came you to call my son out, without explaining your reasons?

Sir Luc. Your son, sir, insulted me in a manner which my honour could not brook.

Sir Anth. Zounds! Jack, how durst you insult the gentleman in a manner which his honour could not brook?

Mrs. Mal. Come, come, let's have no honour before ladies. Captain Absolute, come here. How could you intimidate us so? Here's Lydia has been terrified to death for you.

Abs. For fear I should be killed, or escape, ma'am?

Mrs. Mal. Nay, no delusions to the past—Lydia is convinced; speak, child.

Sir Luc. With your leave, ma'am, I must put in a word here—I believe I could interpret the young lady's silence. Now mark——

Lyd. What is it you mean, sir?

Sir Luc. Come, come, Delia, we must be serious now—this is no time for trifling.

Lyd. 'Tis true, sir; and your reproof bids me offer this gentleman my hand, and solicit the return of his affections.

Abs. Oh! my little angel, say you so? Sir Lucius —I perceive there must be some mistake here, with regard to the affront which you affirm I have given you. I can only say, that it could not have been intentional; and as you must be convinced, that I should not fear to support a real injury, you shall now see that I am not ashamed to atone for an inadvertency— I ask your pardon. But for this lady, while honoured with her approbation, I will support my claim against any man whatever.

Sir Anth. Well said, Jack, and I'll stand by you, my boy.

Acres. Mind, I give up all my claim—I make no pretensions to anything in the world—and if I can't get a wife without fighting for her, by my valour! I'll live a bachelor.

Sir Luc. Captain, give me your hand—an affront handsomely acknowledged becomes an obligation; and as for the lady—if she chooses to deny her own handwriting, here——   [*Takes out letters.*

Mrs. Mal. Oh, he will dissolve my mystery!—Sir Lucius, perhaps there's some mistake—perhaps I can illuminate——

Sir Luc. Pray, old gentlewoman, don't interfere where you have no business. Miss Languish, are you my Delia, or not?

Lyd. Indeed, Sir Lucius, I am not.

[*Lydia and Absolute walk aside.*

Mrs. Mal. Sir Lucius O'Trigger—ungrateful as you are—I own the soft impeachment—pardon my blushes, I am Delia.

Sir Luc. You Delia—pho! pho! be easy.

Mrs. Mal. Why, thou barbarous Vandyke—those letters are mine. When you are more sensible of my benignity, perhaps I may be brought to encourage your addresses.

Sir Luc. Mrs. Malaprop, I am extremely sensible of your condescension; and whether you or Lucy have put this trick upon me, I am equally beholden to you. And, to show you I am not ungrateful, Captain Absolute! since you have taken that lady from me, I'll give you my Delia into the bargain.

Abs. I am much obliged to you, Sir Lucius; but here's my friend, fighting Bob, unprovided for.

Sir Luc. Hah! little Valour—here, will you make your fortune?

Acres. Odds wrinkles! No. But give me your hand, Sir Lucius, forget and forgive; but if ever I give you a chance of *pickling* me again, say Bob Acres is a dunce, that's all.

Sir Anth. Come, Mrs. Malaprop, don't be cast down—you are in your bloom yet.

Mrs. Mal. Oh, Sir Anthony!—men are all barbarians.   [*All retire but* JULIA *and* FAULKLAND.

Jul. He seems dejected and unhappy—not sullen. There was some foundation, however, for the tale he told me. O woman! how true should be your judgement, when your resolution is so weak!

Faulk. Julia!—how can I sue for what I so little deserve? I dare not presume—yet Hope is the child of Penitence.

Jul. O Faulkland, you have not been more faulty in your unkind treatment of me, than I am now in wanting inclination to resent it. As my heart honestly bids me place my weakness to the account of love, I should be ungenerous not to admit the same plea for yours.

Faulk. Now I shall be blest indeed!

[SIR ANTHONY *comes forward.*

Sir Anth. What's going on here? So you have been quarrelling too, I warrant. Come, Julia, I never interfered before; but let me have a hand in the matter at last. All the faults I have ever seen in my friend Faulkland, seemed to proceed from what he calls the delicacy and warmth of his affection for you. There, marry him directly, Julia, you'll find he'll mend surprisingly!   [*The rest come forward.*

Sir Luc. Come now, I hope there is no dissatisfied person, but what is content; for as I have been disappointed myself, it will be very hard if I have not the satisfaction of seeing other people succeed better.

Acres. You are right, Sir Lucius.—So, Jack, I wish you joy—Mr. Faulkland the same. Ladies, come now, to show you I'm neither vexed nor angry, odds tabours and pipes! I'll order the fiddles in half an hour, to the New Rooms—and I insist on your all meeting me there.

Sir Anth. Gad! sir, I like your spirit; and at night we single lads will drink a health to the young couples, and a husband to Mrs. Malaprop.

Faulk. Our partners are stolen from us, Jack—I hope to be congratulated by each other—*yours* for having checked in time the errors of an ill-directed imagination, which might have betrayed an innocent heart ; and *mine*, for having, by her gentleness and candour, reformed the unhappy temper of one, who by it made wretched whom he loved most, and tortured the heart he ought to have adored.

Abs. Well, Jack, we have both tasted the bitters, as well as the sweets, of love—with this difference only, that *you* always prepared the bitter cup for yourself, while *I*——

Lyd. Was always obliged to *me* for it, hey ! Mr. Modesty ?   But come, no more of that—our happiness is now as unalloyed as general.

Jul. Then let us study to preserve it so : and while Hope pictures to us a flattering scene of future bliss, let us deny its pencil those colours which are too bright to be lasting.   When hearts deserving happiness would unite their fortunes, Virtue would crown them with an unfading garland of modest hurtless flowers ; but ill-judging Passion will force the gaudier rose into the wreath, whose thorn offends them when its leaves are dropped !

NOTES

PAGE 2. THE RIVALS. Captain Absolute, Beverley, Bob Acres, and Sir Lucius O'Trigger are all rivals for Lydia's hand.

The play was produced at Covent Garden, January 17, 1775, and at Drury Lane, January 16, 1777.

PROLOGUE

PAGE 3. SERJEANT-AT-LAW. A member of a grade of barristers socially superior but professionally inferior to King's Counsel. They were appointed from members of the Utter or Junior Bar by writ or patent of the Crown. None have been created since 1875. There is now (1912) only one surviving, Lord Lindley.

ATTORNEY. 'Solicitor': barristers can only receive work from solicitors.

1. *cramp.* 'Cramped'.

5–10. The play was withdrawn after the first night: when an amended version was produced eleven days later, these lines were supplanted by the following:

How's this! the poet's brief *again*! O ho!
Cast,[1] I suppose?
    Att. O pardon me—No—No—
We found the court, o'erlooking stricter laws,
Indulgent[2] to the *merits* of the cause;
By *judges* mild, unused to harsh denial,
A rule[3] was granted for *another trial*.
    Serj. Then hark'ee, Dibble, did you *mend* your pleadings?[4]
Errors, no few, we've *found* in our *proceedings*.
    Att. Come, courage, sir, we did *amend* our *plea*,
Hence your *new brief*, and this refreshing fee.[5]

[(1) *Cast*: 'defeated in an action at law'. (2) *Indulgent*, &c.: the Courts of Chancery could afford relief to a suitor, whose cause, though bad in law, was right in equity, i.e. on its merits. (3) *A rule was granted*: the legal phrase for 'permission was given' for another trial. (4) *your pleadings*: the pleadings are all the statements, &c., of both parties which are put into court before the trial so as to decide the exact scope of the dispute: after the trial has begun, special permission is required to alter them. (5) *refreshing fee*, or 'refresher': an extra fee given daily to the barrister if a case is prolonged beyond one day.]

6. *A poet's brief.* The play. A brief is a summary of the facts of a case drawn up by the solicitor for the instruction of the barrister conducting the case in Court.

11. *sons of Phœbus.* 'Poets', sons of Phœbus Apollo, the god of poesy in Greek Myth.: i. e. some barristers are poets.

12. *the Fleet.* The Debtors' Prison on the east side of Farringdon Street. It was pulled down in 1845, the prisoners being removed to the Queen's Bench Prison in Southwark.

14. *bays.* Bay-leaves and laurel are the material of a poet's crown or garland.

his legal waste of wig. The large wig worn by him as a barrister.

15. *Full-bottomed heroes.* Judges and King's Counsel wear full-bottomed wigs (i. e. descending to their shoulders) on state occasions.

signs. 'Painted sign-boards'.

23. *flourish.* 'Use florid language' (Johnson).

PAGE 4. **8.** *No writ of error lies—to Drury Lane.* If we fail here we cannot get a 'writ of error' (i. e. a permission for a new trial on the ground of some unfairness in the circumstances of the first) and have our cause reheard at Drury Lane.

10. *costs of suit.* The winner in a lawsuit can generally recover part of his costs from his opponent.

13. *transportation.* Criminals who escaped the gallows were sentenced to be 'transported' to various places in the British colonies. This punishment was superseded by penal servitude in 1853.

16. *right of challenge.* A party to an action can 'challenge', i. e. object to, any juryman on the ground of incompetency, partiality, &c., and have him struck off the list.

17. *newsman.* Writer of news-letters, or, as we should say, representative of the Press.

PROLOGUE

PAGE 5. *the tenth night.* For a play to have had such a continuous run was in those days a triumph. 'The cause was granted', as the author says.

11. *mask.* Sheridan's MS. and the first and second editions have 'mask', the third has 'masks', which is clearly wrong. The actors in Greek theatres wore masks, differing according to the nature of their drama. Hence certain types of mask became the symbols of Comedy and Tragedy.

23. *The sentimental Muse.* The licentious drama of the

Restoration was succeeded by ' the weeping sentimental comedy ' (Goldsmith, ' An Essay on The Theatre '). Sheridan is never tired of attacking sentimentality whether on the stage or in novels.

Her emblems view. Bunyan's *Pilgrim's Progress* and rue, the ' sour herb of grace ' (Shakespeare, *Richard II*, III. iv), are emblems of the severe morality of the Sentimental Comedy.

26. *on emblematic wood,* i. e. she is wooden, lifeless.

28. *the dagger from her sister's hand.* Melpomene, the Muse of Tragedy, whose emblem is a dagger.

PAGE 6. 1. *Harry Woodward,* &c. See Dramatis Personae, p. 2.

EPILOGUE

PAGE 7. 9. *the Cit.* ' The Citizen ' = ' cockney '.

11. *John Trot.* A proverbial name for a boor or uncultured person; perhaps from ' John Trott ', the pretended author of Steele's papers, *Spectator* (1712) 296, 314, who, however, was merely ' awkward '.

14. *Zounds.* For ' 'swounds ' = ' God's wounds ', those of Christ upon the cross ; a common oath.

15. *the vanquished victor.* See Dryden, *Alexander's Feast,* l. 97.

17. *blade.* A gallant free-and-easy fellow ; probably from blade, ' a sword ', but whether figuratively or as wielder of a blade is uncertain.

19. *bumpers.* Glasses of wine, filled to the brim.

PAGE 8. 9. *fairly.* ' Honourably '.

24. *beaux.* ' Dandies ' : Fr. beau, *f.* belle, ' beautiful .

ACT I

SCENE I

PAGE 9. 3. *Odds life.* An oath, ' God's life '. Od's, Ad's, Ud's, &c., are other seventeenth- and eighteenth-century corruptions of ' God ' to disguise the profaneness of the oaths.

7. *as hearty.* Slang for ' as hearty as can be imagined ' or some such phrase.

9. *Harry, Mrs. Kate.* Presumably servants of Sir Anthony.

10. *postilion.* The rider of the near horse in an old-fashioned carriage or post-chaise.

14. *gi't.* ' Give it '.

19. *Odd.* See l. 3 n.

22. *Ensign.* ' Sub-lieutenant ' : the commissioned officers of

the lowest grade in the infantry used to carry the ensign or standard.

23. *doubt.* 'Fear'.

PAGE 10. 14. *a masquerader . . . Jupiter.* Jupiter or Zeus, the chief of the gods in classical mythology, put on various forms in his pursuits of mortal maidens, a shower of gold (Danae), a satyr (Antiope), a swan (Leda), a bull (Europa), &c.

21. *half-pay ensign.* Officers not on actual service receive only half their pay.

27. *the stocks.* In 1751 a great variety of loans to the Government had been consolidated into a single stock, at a uniform rate of interest. They are now known as Consols.

30. *thread-papers.* Strips of paper folded in creases so as to form separate divisions for different skeins of thread, the paper so folded forming a long and narrow strip.

33. *a set of thousands.* What does this mean ? Nettleton explains 'a team of six horses worth thousands of pounds', and quotes 'A most rich Coach and Curious Sett of Six horses' from Ashton's *Social Life in the Reign of Queen Anne*, I. iii. But a 'set of thousands' would mean, by analogy, a set of thousands of horses, and no coachman would speak enthusiastically of such a handful. On the other hand it can hardly be a 'set' of stocks. Could it be 'following' or 'society', as we say 'in his set', 'among your set'? The Coachman suggests, as an impediment to Captain Absolute's suit, that he is only one of thousands who run after her.

draw . . . with. Cf. 'pull together with', both metaphors from beasts of draught = 'agree with'.

PAGE 11. 4. *mort.* 'A great deal'. Common in most Irish and English dialects for 'a large quantity' or 'a great number': its origin is uncertain.

6. *lounge.* 'Place for lounging'.

pump-room. The room where the medicinal waters, which were the presumed object of visitors to Bath, were supplied by pumping from cisterns.

11. *not a fiddle nor a card after eleven.* Some of the tyrannical authority of Beau Nash, who first exploited Bath as a fashionable resort, descended to his successors as Masters of the Ceremonies.

12. *gentleman*, i. e. valet.

keep it up. 'Keep up the amusement'; slang.

15. *Mr. Du-Peign.* The correct spelling is Du-Peigne, p. 25, l. 21. Cf. Mr. De-la-grace (p. 53, l. 18). It was fashionable to keep a French valet.

20. *ton.* Fr. = 'tone', hence 'fashion'.

24. *took to their own hair.* Left off wearing wigs.

25. *Odd rabbit it.* A quite meaningless oath, probably a facetious alteration of ' Od rat (i. e. rot) it ', which now survives as ' Drat it '.

when the fashion, &c. The Bar = both the lawyers, and the bar of the carriage on which one steps in mounting to the Box. The Box is the coachman's seat.

33. *thoff.* ' Though '.

Jack Gauge. An exciseman (or revenue officer) gauges or measures the contents of casks.

ta'en to his carrots. Wears his own red hair ; see l. 24 n.

35. *bob.* ' Bob-wig ', a wig with the bottom locks of hair turned up into ' bobs ' or short curls.

the college. The College of Physicians, or the College of Surgeons, to one of which all qualified doctors belong.

39. *Zooks.* ' Gadszooks '; an oath, probably quite meaningless.

PAGE 12. 7. *Gyde's Porch.* The porch to the Lower (Assembly) Rooms kept by Mr. Gyde.

SCENE II

12. *The Reward of Constancy.* Perhaps *Female Constancy ; or, The History of Miss Arabella Waldegrave,* 2 vols. (1769). This is the only item in Lydia's sentimental library which has not been traced by Mr. Nettleton in his edition of 1906.

15. *The Fatal Connexion.* By Mrs. Fogerty (1773).

17. *The Mistakes of the Heart. Or, Memoirs of Lady Caroline Pelham and Lady Victoria Nevil,* by de Vergy Treysac, 4 vols. (1772).

18. *Mr. Bull.* Lewis Bull, a Bath bookseller.

20. *The Delicate Distress.* Published (1769–70) by Mrs. Elizabeth Griffith (d. 1793), as companion to *The Gordian Knot;* by her husband Richard Griffith (d. 1788).

22. *The Memoirs of Lady Woodford.* Reviewed in *The Monthly Review,* 1771.

24. *Mr. Frederick.* A bookseller at Bath from 1745 to 1772.

PAGE 13. 1. *The Gordian Knot.* See p. 12, l. 20 n.

Peregrine Pickle. The Adventures of Peregrine Pickle, including *The Memoirs of a Lady of Quality* (1751), and *The Expedition of Humphrey Clinker* (1771), are by Tobias Smollett (1721–71), one of the great novelists of the eighteenth century.

2. *The Tears of Sensibility.* Four novels translated from the French of M. D'Arnaud (1716–1805) by John Murdoch (1773).

4. *The Sentimental Journey. A Sentimental Journey through*

France and Italy (1768), by Laurence Sterne (1713-68), the author of *Tristram Shandy*.

8. *The Whole Duty of Man.* Published anonymously in 1659 : more than forty editions were issued in the next two hundred years. There was also a *New Whole Duty* (1744), which had reached its twenty-third edition by 1773.

9. *blonds.* Blond, or blonde lace, was lace made of unbleached silk.

10. *sal volatile.* 'Volatile salt': doctors' Latin for a solution of ammonium carbonate used as a restorative in fainting fits.

17. *Miss Melville.* Julia is only under the voluntary protection of Sir Anthony; see p. 15, l. 15.

28. *Mrs. Malaprop.* From Fr. *mal* (ill) + *à* (to) + *propos* (purpose) = 'inappropriate'. Her distinguishing feature (see p. 16, l. 24) was taken by Sheridan from Mrs. Tryfort in his mother's unacted comedy, *A Journey to Bath.*

PAGE 14. 1. *a tall Irish baronet.* Irishmen in eighteenth-century fiction are nearly always penniless adventurers.

3. *rout.* A large evening party or reception (eighteenth and early nineteenth century).

8. *a Delia or a Celia.* Two names much used by seventeenth-century poets to conceal the identity of their mistresses.

PAGE 15. 10. *à propos.* Lit. 'to the purpose' (p. 13, l. 28 n.), i. e. with regard to the subject under discussion.

PAGE 16. 24. *with her select words,* &c. Cf. the description of Mrs. Tryfort, undoubtedly the prototype of Mrs. Malaprop, in Mrs. Sheridan's comedy *A Journey to Bath,* I. v. ' 'Tis the vainest poor creature, and the fondest of hard words, which without miscalling, she always takes care to misapply.'

Mrs. Malaprop's mistakes are of two kinds. Most frequently she uses a word which bears some resemblance to the word intended, but sometimes her words are merely high-sounding, without any such resemblance. In other cases it is doubtful whether a malapropism is intended, i. e. the obvious meaning of the words, though unexpected, is not totally irrelevant, and in others again the words could, but do not usually, bear the meaning necessary to the passage.

27. *coz.* 'Cousin'.

34. *Roderick Random.* By Smollett; see p. 5, l. 23 n.

The Innocent Adultery. A translation of *L'Adultère Innocente,* by Paul Scarron (1610-60), the French novelist, husband of Madame de Maintenon. There were many English editions of his works.

PAGE 17. 1. *Lord Aimworth.* Probably '*The History of Lord*

Aimsworth, and the honourable Charles Hartford, Esq., in a series of letters. A novel in three volumes by the author of *Dorinda Catsby*, &c.'; see *The Gentleman's Magazine*, May 1773.

2. *Ovid.* The Roman poet (43 B. C.–A. D. 17); translations of his poems, which are mostly love-stories, were very popular in the eighteenth century.

3. *The Man of Feeling.* By the Scottish novelist and dramatist Henry Mackenzie (1745–1831), called by Scott the ' Northern Addison '. It was published in 1771.

4. *Mrs. Chapone.* Hester Chapone (1727–1801) wrote a book of essays, *Letters on the Improvement of the Mind* (1773), for the benefit of a niece.

    Fordyce's Sermons. James Fordyce (1720–96), a Presbyterian divine, published *Sermons to Young Women* (1765), which ran through many editions.

6. *the hairdresser has torn away.* To serve as curl-papers, &c.

8. *Lord Chesterfield's Letters.* Philip Stanhope (1694–1773), fourth Earl of Chesterfield, wrote a series of letters to his natural son instructing him how to become a ' man of the world '. They were published by the son's widow in 1774.

18. *illiterate.* For ' obliterate '.

32. *extirpate.* For ' exculpate '.

33. *controvertible.* For ' incontrovertible '.

PAGE 18. 21. *intricate.* For ' obstinate ' or, perhaps,' intriguing '.

25. *the black art.* Magic.

28. *misanthropy.* For ' misanthrope '.

32. *half-bound volumes, with marble covers.* The backs and corners were bound in leather, and the sides were of marbled paper, i. e. coloured to resemble certain marbles.

37. *an ever-green tree,* &c. Cf. ' the tree of the knowledge of good and evil ', Gen. ii. 17.

PAGE 19. 2. *laconically.* For ' ironically '.

5. *Observe me.* ' Pay attention to me '; *obs.*

6. *progeny.* For ' prodigy '.

9. *Simony, or Fluxions, or Paradoxes.* See p. 16, l. 24 n. Mrs. Malaprop has heard the words and thinks they are names of branches of learning. Simony is the sin of trafficking in sacred things, especially the buying or selling of ecclesiastical preferment : Simon Magus (Acts viii. 9–24) wished to purchase the gift of the Holy Ghost with money. Fluxions (*lit.* flowings) is a mathematical term used in the calculus.

13. *diabolical.* See p. 16, l. 24 n.

16. *supercilious.* For ' superficial '.

18. *geometry.* For ' geography '.

19. *contagious.* For ' contiguous '.
20. *orthodoxy.* For ' orthography '.
23. *reprehend.* For ' apprehend '.
25. *superstitious.* For ' superfluous '.

PAGE 20. 14. *illegible.* For ' ineligible '.
18. *keep a tight hand.* So. ' on the reins ', a metaphor from driving.
22. *come about.* ' Come round ', ' change her mind '.
24. *intuition.* For ' tuition '.
28. *artificial.* For ' artful '.
32. *you was.* A fashionable perversion of ' you were '.
36. *Gemini.* The Great Twin (Lat. *gemini*) Brethren, Castor and Pollux, or the constellation called after them : here a mild oath. (The oath is possibly a corruption of *Jesu domine.*)

PAGE 21. 6. *malevolence.* For ' benevolence '.
7. *locality.* For ' loquacity ' = talkativeness.
23. *paduasoy.* A garment of Paduasoy, probably a corruption of ' Padua say ', i. e. ' say ' or serge brought from Padua, a city near Venice.
26. *pocket-pieces.* Pieces of money, generally out of currency or spurious or damaged, carried in the pocket as charms.
28. *Hibernian.* ' Irishman ' : Lat. *Hibernia* = Ireland.

ACT II

SCENE I

PAGE 22. 7. *interjectural.* For ' parenthetical '.
20. *'Sdeath !* God's death.
23. *sly, sir—devilish sly.* Dickens adopted this as the catch-phrase of Joey Bagstock in *Dombey and Son.*
31. *chairmen.* Carriers of the Sedan chairs, closed vehicles to seat one person, borne on two poles by bearers, one in front and one behind. The wheeled Bath chair is of later invention.
32. *minority waiters.* A discussion of this phrase in *Notes and Queries,* 6th Ser., leaves the meaning still doubtful; probably here = persons waiting for a government appointment, which, however, they despair of obtaining, as their party is in a minority. —*N.E.D.*

PAGE 23. 1. *whenever I draw,* &c. In a *bill* A (here Fag), who signs or *draws* it, requests B (here his *invention*) to pay C a sum of money (here *a good current lie*), generally at some future date. If C requires money immediately, he may sell the *bill* for a smaller sum to any other person, who may, however, require C to *endorse* it, i. e. to sign his name on the back, whereby he becomes security for the payment of the bill, if B and A refuse.

3 *take care you don't hurt your credit*, &c. All Fag's details are additional security for his first statement. Absolute warns him that his credit will suffer, if he thinks it necessary to offer so much security.

PAGE 24. 8. *reversion*. The right of succession on the death of the present holder.

21. *farrago*. 'Medley', 'mixture'; Lat. = 'mixed fodder for cattle'.

PAGE 25. 4. *aspiration*. 'Breath'; Lat. *aspirare*, to breathe upon.

PAGE 26. 5. *Odds whips and wheels*. For Acres's *oaths referential*, see p. 30, l. 26 sqq.

7. *the Mall*. A gravel walk on the north side of St. James's Park, from Constitution Hill to Spring Gardens, which has now developed into the broad processional road. In the eighteenth century it was the fashionable evening lounge.

13. *solicit your connexions*. 'Beg to have acquaintance with you'.

23. *the German Spa*. Spa is a watering-place in Belgium: hence its name was given to watering-places in other countries.

PAGE 27. 6. *odds crickets*. See p. 26, l. 5 n. Crickets are proverbially 'merry and gay'.

29. *harpsichord*. A musical instrument shaped like a grand piano, but sounding more like a harp; in general use from the sixteenth to the eighteenth century.

30. *squallante, rumblante*, &c. 'Squalling, rumbling, and quivering'. Acres coins these words in imitation of the Italian (*andante*, &c.) habitually used in music.

32. *odds minnums and crotchets*. In music minims are notes of half the value, and crotchets are notes of quarter the value of a semibreve.

37. '*music the food of love*'. Cf. Shak., *Twelfth Night*, I. i. 'If music be the food of love, play on.'

PAGE 28. 3. *purling-stream airs*. Tunes that sound like the 'purling' or 'murmuring' of running water, i. e. sentimental.

4. *When absent from my soul's delight*. Mr. Nettleton 'after prolonged, but fruitless search', could find no song closer to this than 'When absent from the nymph I love' in *Calliope : or the Vocal Enchantress*, London (1788), p. 176.

7. *Go, gentle gales !* The refrain of *The Faithful Lover*, set to

music by Dr. Arne; see *Clio and Euterpe or British Harmony* (1762), vol. iii, p. 1.

9. *My heart's my own*, &c. From *Love in a Village* (1762), I. i, a comic opera by Isaac Bickerstaffe (d. 1812 ?).

PAGE 29. 3. *minuet*. A slow stately dance for two persons, very fashionable in the eighteenth century.

6. *country dancing*. English dances of rural origin, especially those in which an indefinite number of couples stand up face to face, as in the *Roger de Coverley*.

odds swimmings ! 'Swims' are smooth 'swaying', gliding motions in dancing.

13. *Z—ds !* Zounds = 'God's wounds', i. e. Christ's on the cross.

14. *cotillion*. More properly 'cotillon', from Fr. *cotillon*, a petticoat : the name of several French dances, generally more dignified than the country dances.

16. *palming*. Handling. In many English dances, as for instance, the Lancers, each lady gives her hand to each gentleman in turn.

17. *a managed filly*. A filly learning or having learnt the *manège*, the various actions and paces taught in a riding-school.

27. *impregnate*. Fill with their influence.

31. *looby*. 'Lout' : cf. 'lubber'.

PAGE 30. 11. *odds frogs and tambours*. *Frogs* were ornamental fastenings for the front of a military coat : *tambours* (Fr. *tambour*, 'drum') were pieces of embroidery, so called from the circular frames on which the silk was stretched for the purpose of being embroidered. For the system of swearing see below, l. 26 sq.

12. *ancient madam*. Acres's mother. She is called 'the old lady' elsewhere (p. 53, l. 6, and p. 57, l. 21).

14. *cashier*. 'Dismiss from service', a military term.

15. *incapable*. Sc. 'of being worn any longer'.

18. *thoff*. See p. 11, l. 33 n.

22. *flints*. Eighteenth-century guns were fitted with locks in which a flint was struck against the hammer and produced sparks which ignited the powder.

28. *militia*. The force raised in each county by the Lord-Lieutenant, in which every able-bodied citizen was liable to do fourteen days' training in each year.

35. *the 'oath should be an echo to the sense'*. Cf. 'The sound must seem an echo to the sense—', Pope's *Essay on Criticism*, l. 365.

PAGE 31. 15. *give me a dozen bumpers*, &c., i. e. drink her health a dozen times, to oblige me : see p. 7, l. 19 n.

PAGE 33. 15. *my vows are pledged*, &c. To *pledge* anything is to make it security for borrowed money. If the money is not repaid, i. e. the pledge not *redeemed*, within a certain time, the lender can *foreclose*, i. e. bar the right of redemption, and treat the pledge as his absolute property.

PAGE 34. 1. *the Crescent.* The Royal Crescent, Bath, begun 1767.

2. *the bull's in Cox's Museum.* James Cox was a London mechanician, who exhibited fifty-six mechanical curiosities at Spring Gardens in 1774–5. Two or three 'pieces' had bulls in them, but there is no record of their 'rolling eye'.

39. *a five-and-threepence.* Probably a sum taken at random for a legal fee, being a quarter of a guinea. But cf. the modern 'six-and-eightpence'.

PAGE 35. 1. *unget.* 'Unbeget'.

16. *turnspit.* The cook's dog, of a small, long-bodied and short-legged species, used to work a kind of treadwheel by which a spit was turned.

17. *triumvirate.* A body of three men. It was the Roman custom to call commissioners for any public purpose *duumviri, triumviri, decemviri,* &c., according to the number of the commissioners.

22. *trims.* 'Dresses down', as we now say.

SCENE II

PAGE 36. 6. *till my purse . . . form.* Till I've been properly bribed.

11. *Dalia.* She mimics the Irishman's pronunciation of Delia.

18. *O Gemini !* See p. 20, l. 36 n.

PAGE 37. 2. *incentive.* For 'instinctive'.

3. *induction.* For 'seduction'.

4. *combination.* See p. 16, l. 24 n.

5. *superfluous.* For 'superficial'.

6. *punctuation.* For 'punctilio'.

8. *infallible.* For 'ineffable'.

criterion. See p. 16, l. 24 n.

22. *pressed.* To 'press' or 'impress' was to force a man to serve in the army or navy.

23. *get their habeas corpus.* 'Be set at liberty'. A *habeas corpus* (Lat. 'thou mayest have the body') is a writ requiring a person in detention to be brought before the judge, so that the lawfulness of the detention may be investigated.

31. *nice.* 'Dainty', 'particular'.

PAGE 38. 2. *gemman.* For 'gentleman'.

20. *call . . . out.* 'Challenge to a duel.'

ACT III

Scene I

Page 39. 20. *getting.* ' Begetting '; cf. p. 35, l. 1 n.

Page 41. 39. *phlegmatic.* Cold and unenthusiastic. In old physiology phlegm was one of the four bodily ' humours ', and indolence or apathy was the sign of its prevalence in the body.

40. *anchorite.* Hermit.

stock. A wooden block.

Page 42. 1. *block*, i. e. a piece of wood on which the uniforms were beaten to rid them of dust.

22. *the Promethian torch.* (Erron. for *Promethean* ;) ' the principle of life '. In Greek myth. the Titan Prometheus made men of clay and stole fire from heaven to animate them. For this Zeus chained him to Mount Caucasus, where an eagle preyed daily on his liver.

Scene II

Page 44. 13. *veering but a point.* A point is one of the thirty-two points of the mariner's compass, each representing 11° 15′.

17. *title to your gratitude.* See p. 16.

Scene III

Page 46. 14. *accommodation.* For ' recommendation '.

15. *ingenuity.* For ' ingenuousness '.

25. *ineffectual.* For ' intellectual '.

35. *the orange-tree.* Its flowers and fruit are often seen together.

Page 47. 2. *pine-apple.* For ' pinnacle ', perhaps, but see p. 16, l. 24 n.

5. *strolling.* ' Vagabond ', used esp. of itinerant performers.

11. *exploded.* See p. 16, l. 24 n.

12. *conjunctions.* For ' injunctions '.

13. *preposition.* For ' proposition '.

15. *particle.* Perhaps for ' article ', but see p. 16, l. 24 n.

17. *hydrostatics.* For ' hysterics '.

18. *persisted.* For ' desisted '.

20. *interceded.* For ' intercepted '.

Page 48. 17. *reprehend.* For ' comprehend '.

18. *oracular.* For ' vernacular '.

derangement. For ' arrangement '.

epitaphs. For ' epithets '.

25. *coxcomb.* A ' pretentious fool ', from the cap worn by a professional fool, shaped and coloured like a cock's comb.

26. *harridan.* 'An ill-tempered old woman': deriv. uncertain.
39. *laid by the heels.* Orig. 'put in irons or the stocks', hence 'overthrown'.

PAGE 49. **2.** *perpetrated.* See p. 16, l. 24 n.

PAGE 51. **34.** *contain.* For 'contain myself', a very rare use.

PAGE 52. **4.** *allegory.* For 'alligator'.
14. *stroller.* See p. 47, l. 5 n.

SCENE IV

PAGE 53. **1.** *an'.* 'If'.
2. *monkerony.* For 'macaroni', from 1760–80 a common term for a dandy, derived from the Macaroni Club, which was probably so called to indicate its preference for foreign cooking. At that date macaroni had hardly reached England from Italy : the art of cooking it has not yet arrived.
6. *Clod Hall.* Acres's home in Devonshire.
12. *Oons!* The same as 'Zounds'; see p. 7, l. 14 n.
I'll hold a gallon, &c. 'I'll bet a gallon' the dogs don't recognize you.
18. *Mr. De-la-grace.* See p. 11, l. 15 n.
19. *balancing, and chasing, and boring.* Various movements in dancing.
27. *Sink, slide, coupee.* Other movements in dancing.
28. *cotillons.* See p. 29, l. 14 n.
29. *minuet.* See p. 29, l. 3 n.
31. *stick.* Generally used of a stiff and awkward performer : very rare in this sense.
country-dance. See p. 29, l. 9 n.
32. *tabours.* Small drums.
cross-over to couple, &c. Movements in country-dances, which he had never thought difficult ('valued').
35. *allemandes.* German (Fr. 'allemande') dances of moderate rapidity, in common time.
38. *pas . . . Paws.* Fr. for 'step': Acres's pronunciation is thoroughly English.

PAGE 54. **2.** *Antigallican.* 'Opposed to what is French'.
10. *Jack-a-lantern.* The 'will-o'-the-wisp', or ignis fatuus, the flame of burning marsh-gas.
33. *We wear no swords here.* The wearing of swords had been prohibited by Beau Nash owing to the frequency of duels, and the prohibition was continued by his successors.

PAGE 55. **18.** *Achilles.* The Greek hero, see Homer's *Iliad*, *passim.*

19. *little.* Probably a term of affection : cf. 'poor little dear Sir Lucius', p. 80, l. 32.

Alexander the Great. (356–323 B. C.) King of Macedon.

20. *broad-swords.* Cutting swords with broad blades.

26. *pans.* In ancient guns the *pan* is the part of the lock which holds the powder.

30. *the new room.* The new Assembly Rooms of 1771.

36. *militia.* See p. 30, l. 28 n.

38. *the milk of human kindness.* Shak., *Macbeth*, I. v.

40. ' *I could do such deeds——*'. In *N. & Q.*, 8th ser., ix. 247, it is suggested that Acres is misquoting

> Now could I drink hot blood,
> And do such bitter business, &c.
>
> Shak., Hamlet III. ii.

ACT IV

SCENE I

PAGE 57. 19. *Oons!* Identical with 'Zounds'; see p. 7, l. 14 n.

25. *bloodthirsty cormorants.* The cormorant, a large sea-bird, is proverbial for its voracity.

27. *quarter-staff, or short-staff.* The quarter-staff was a stout pole, from six to eight feet long and tipped with iron, formerly used as a weapon by the English peasantry : the sense of 'quarter' is uncertain. The short-staff is any cudgel.

29. *sharps and snaps.* Swords and pistols.

PAGE 60. 22. *my second.* It would not be proper for Absolute to act, as he is thought to be a friend of Acres's opponent, Beverley.

SCENE II

PAGE 61. 23. *caparisons.* For 'comparisons'.

27. *alacrity and adulation.* See p. 16, l. 24 n.

30. *grammatical.* See p. 16, l. 24 n.

31. *what Hamlet says.*

> Hyperion's curls ; the front of Jove himself ;
> An eye like Mars, to threaten and command ;
> A station, like the herald Mercury
> New lighted on a heaven-kissing hill.
>
> Shak., Hamlet, III. iv.

Hyperion is the Sun : used by Shakespeare as identical with Apollo. A *station* = ' a way of standing '.

PAGE 62. 1. *similitude.* For ' simile '.

PAGE 63. 3. *affluence.* For ' influence '.

36. *quinsy.* Inflammation of the throat.

PAGE 64. 31. *Bedlam.* The priory of St. Mary of Bethlehem in London (popularly known as Bedlam) was given to the city in 1547 and transformed into a lunatic asylum.

PAGE 65. 36. *compilation.* For ' appellation '.

PAGE 66. 4. *clever.* In obs. sense ' convenient ', ' agreeable '.

8. *anticipate . . . retrospection.* Mrs. Malaprop says she will not look forward to the past, nor backward to the future.

15. ' *Youth 's the season made for joy* '. A song in Gay's *Beggar's Opera* (1727), II.

PAGE 68. 18. *analysed.* For ' paralysed '.

25. *Cerberus.* Pluto's dog, stationed at the entrance of Hades, to prevent the living passing in or the dead passing out. According to most mythologists he had three heads.

SCENE III

PAGE 69. 27. *the old serpent.* The Tempter of Gen. iii.

28. *caught, like vipers,* &c. Vipers are said to attack a piece of red cloth with such fury that they expend all their venom on it, and can then be handled without danger.

PAGE 71. 10. *pother.* ' Fuss '. In the eighteenth century it rhymed with ' other ', but now has been assimilated to ' bother '.

20. *small-sword.* The light sword used for fencing with the point only.

PAGE 73. 10. ' *not unsought be won.* ' See Milton, *Par. Lost,* viii. 502–3 :

> Her virtue, and the conscience of her worth,
> That would be wooed, and not unsought be won.

26. *touchstone.* ' A very fine-grained dark-coloured variety of schist or jasper, used for trying the quality of alloys of the precious metals. The alloy is rubbed on the stone, and the colour of the streak is compared with that of various alloys of known composition prepared for that purpose and called *touch-needles* ' (*The Century Dictionary*).

28. *sterling.* ' Pure ': orig. of money = ' conforming to the national standard of value '.

ACT V

Scene I

Page 76. 19. *forbid.* Obs. pa. pple., now 'forbidden'.

Page 77. 19. *the moon's...idiots...madness.* The prevalence of the superstition that madness is caused by the influence of the moon is shown in the word 'lunatic' from Lat. *luna,* the moon.

Page 78. 15. *a mere Smithfield bargain.* Bought and sold like cattle at the Smithfield cattle-market, abolished in 1855. Apparently wives were sometimes bartered at this market.

18. *conscious.* In its Latin sense of 'privy to' or 'sharing in' a human action, from *con* (with)+ *scio* (know).

four horses—Scotch parson. After 1754 it was impossible for minors to be married in England without the parents' or guardians' consent. Hence many young couples ran away to Scotland, where a legal marriage could be effected merely by the two parties declaring their wish to marry in the presence of witnesses. At Gretna Green, the nearest Scottish village, the toll-keeper alone married two hundred couples in a year.

24. *a bishop's licence.* A licence in place of banns can be granted by a bishop for the solemnization of a marriage in the church of a parish in which one of the parties resides.

Page 79. 11. *suicide, paracide.* See p. 16, l. 24 n. 'Paracide' is an erroneous form of 'parricide'.

simulation. See p. 16, l. 24 n.

13. *antistrophe.* For 'catastrophe'. An antistrophe is part of an ode.

17. *enveloped.* See p. 16, l. 24 n.

26. *flourishing.* See p. 3, l. 23 n.

32. *perpendiculars.* For 'particulars'.

Page 80. 15. *firearms, firelocks,* &c. Any compound of 'fire' seems to David in his excitement to be a weapon. A firelock is a form of gun in which sparks were produced by friction or percussion to ignite the powder. A fire-office is the office of a fire-insurance company.

16. *crackers.* Fireworks.

27. *participate.* For 'precipitate'.

29. *given.* 'Disposed': *N.E.D.* treats this use of 'given' (cf. 'well given', 'devoutly given') as identical with 'given to' ('given to excesses, to evil', &c.).

30. *Philistine.* In the eighteenth century applied to drunken and debauched persons, and also to any 'enemy', e.g. bailiffs,

literary critics, &c., into whose hands one might fall. Here perhaps the reference is to the warlike qualities of the ancient Philistines. The modern sense of ' uncultured, unenlightened' originated in the nineteenth century.

34. *petrefactions.* The early editions have ' putrifactions', an excellent Malapropism for ' petrefactions '. In the limestone rocks of Derbyshire there are plentiful fossilized remains.

36. *felicity.* For ' velocity '.

PAGE 81. 1. *exhort.* For ' escort '.

2. *envoy.* For ' convoy '.

3. *precede.* See p. 16, l. 24 n.

SCENE II

10. *A sword seen,* &c. See p. 54, l. 33 n.
takes a circle. Turns round.

PAGE 83. 34. *beadles.* Inferior parish officers who kept order in church, punished petty offenders, and acted as general servants of the parish.

36. *give me your shoulder.* Sir Anthony has the gout ; see p. 9, l. 12.

SCENE III

PAGE 84. 32. *quietus.* ' Discharge ': short for ' Quietus est' med. Lat. = ' he is quit ', i. e. his accounts have been settled.

PAGE 85. 1. *pickled,* i. e. ' embalmed '.

3. *the Abbey.* The Abbey Church at Bath.

very snug lying. ' A deplorable account of the sanitary condition of the Abbey at this time is given in *The New Prose Bath Guide for 1778,* p. 30, showing the danger of attending divine service there ' (Knight).

13. *Odds files.* This oath does not seem very appropriate here. The ' files ' intended must be military ' files ', i. e. the number of men constituting the depth from front to rear of a military formation.

23. *of its own head.* Of its own accord.

37. *lieve.* Generally ' lief ' = ' gladly '.

PAGE 86. 24. *doubt.* ' Fear '.

PAGE 88. 38. *I serve his majesty.* As an officer in the army Absolute could not refuse a challenge.

PAGE 89. 18. *delusions.* For ' allusions '.

19. *convinced.* See p. 16, l. 24 n.

PAGE 90. 9. *dissolve.* For ' solve '.

20. *Vandyke.* For 'Vandal' : the Teutonic tribe, which plundered Rome in the fifth century A. D., is proverbial for its barbarity. Vandyke was a celebrated Flemish painter, who came to England in 1632 and painted the chief persons of Charles I's Court.

PAGE 91. 33. *the New Rooms.* See p. 55, l. 30 n.
36. *we single lads.* It does not appear that Sir Anthony was a widower ; see p. 65, l. 2.
38. *are stolen.* ' Have stolen away, departed quietly '.

PAGE 92. 20. *but ill-judging Passion.* Note that Sheridan ends with two and a half lines of blank verse.

PRINTED IN GREAT BRITAIN
AT THE UNIVERSITY PRESS, OXFORD
BY VIVIAN RIDLER
PRINTER TO THE UNIVERSITY